MW01233165

EFFECTIVE POSITIVE REINFORCEMENT DOG TRAINING

TRANSFORM BEHAVIOR AND BUILD TRUST—EVEN
FOR BUSY OWNERS

SANDRA FELLERS

CONTENTS

INTRODUCTION

> When the dog looks at you, the dog is not thinking
> what kind of a person you are. The dog is not
> judging you.
>
> — ECKHART TOLLE

Imagine a being with an endless capacity for love, acceptance, joy, and forgiveness. Imagine a loyalty that couldn't be rivaled by anyone else, accompanied by an undying need to make you happy. A companion that never judges you and listens to every word that you say with a sparkle in their eyes. They want to be with you every chance that they can get and will never grow tired of your presence. Now, put all of this in a furry body with four legs and a wagging tail, and you've got yourself a dog!

Dogs truly are special creatures, and that's why we all know them as man's best friend. They have the potential to be the perfect companions with their willingness to learn, their natural curiosity, and their overall playful nature. No wonder dogs have been a part of human history for more than 30,000 years (Yong, 2016).

We can create meaningful, loving, and lasting bonds with our canine friends if we have the right tools to do so. All of us love animals, and having a dog as a companion is an aspiration for many. However, there are cases where dogs can start to cause problems in the household. Don't get me wrong, there is no such thing as a bad dog! Unfortunately, because dogs are very intelligent creatures, they can quickly learn bad behaviors if left to their own devices.

Therefore, to ensure that our dogs can help us form a happy family, we have to intervene. Training your dog effectively can save you so much heartache and bad experiences in the future. However, sometimes we may feel like we don't have the time or knowledge to train our dogs well, and it might even make us feel guilty. Perhaps you've tried countless orthodox training methods, and it has just felt pointless since the day you started.

I vividly remember the day my mother surprised me with a beautiful black Labrador puppy two weeks shy of my sixteenth birthday. I remember the smell of puppy breath grazing my cheek as I swooped him up and squeezed him against my chest. I was more than thrilled, especially since I had a birthday party planned with all of my friends. This would allow me to show off the most adorable little creature that I've ever seen!

On that fateful day, we were all gathered around the table by the pool, and my mother had just brought out the cake while starting a chorus of Happy Birthday. I was in my happy place with all of my loved ones around me, and a jumpy new little friend in my arms. My mother placed the cake on the table in front of me, and kissed me on the cheek, encouraging me to make a wish.

As I bent over and blew out the candles, I released my grip on Bear ever so slightly for a split second. This was more than enough time for him to launch out of my arms facefirst into the large cake that my mother had spent hours baking. Everyone watched in horror as I fished him out of the icing. Bear thanked my mother for the cake later that day by leaving her a warm present on her brand-new carpet right before the guests started leaving. Perfect timing, of course.

I was quite embarrassed by Bear's behavior that day, which moved me to start researching dog training. Dogs acting out in public can be mortifying to their owners. Trust me, I've been there. Effective training can help you avoid such instances, and perhaps a few glares from someone who has just bought a new carpet. Some dogs may have difficulty overcoming specific issues, such as excessive barking, chewing on shoes, separation anxiety, or even aggression. If these problems are severe, they can have a significant impact on your relationship with your dog and others in your household.

Positive reinforcement dog training is the answer. Forget everything that you've learned about taking a dominance or punishment-based approach. Positive reinforcement training focuses on building the relationship between pet and owner, establishing trust, and rewarding good behavior. By taking this approach, we can encourage the behavior that we want to see in our dogs without having to shout at, spank, or scare them. This kind of negative reinforcement may lead to distrust, fear, and aggression.

In this book, we'll be going over everything that you need to know about training your dog and doing it consistently, even with a limited amount of time. Whether you're a very busy individual with a tight schedule or someone who has a little bit more time to spare in their day, these training techniques will be a life-changer for you and your pet.

We'll be looking at all of your dog's needs, potty training, leash training, socializing, excessive anxiety and aggression, commands, and so much more. After reading this book, you will have all of the necessary information and confidence to create a happy and harmonious relationship with your pet.

I have spent decades working closely with dogs from all kinds of backgrounds, and I have personally seen the change that the correct training can make in the lives of dogs and their owners. My mission is to get all of this crucial information to as many dog owners as possible to help them unleash the potential that their beautiful companions hold and improve their quality of life.

This journey is all about learning and getting to know your dog in a way that you would have never thought possible. As we learn what their needs are and how to work with them, we can grow with them. Positive reinforcement training is not only about changing the pet's behavior but also changing the owner's mindset. We learn just as much from this method of dog training as they do, which is why it is so effective. Although taking up such a responsibility may seem daunting, I will be here to guide you every step of the way. An obedient, well-behaved dog is well within reach! Let's take the first step of this journey together.

1

LAYING THE FOUNDATION

> *The great pleasure of a dog is that you may make a fool of yourself with him and not only will he not scold you, but he will make a fool of himself too.*
>
> — SAMUEL BUTLER

In order to build a trusting relationship with our canine companions, it's paramount that we understand the basics. The right information makes the world's difference. I have seen numerous instances where pet owners fail to efficiently train their dogs due to a lack of basic necessary information. Even the perfect training regimen can prove ineffective if your pet's needs aren't met.

In this chapter, we'll be going over everything you need to know about caring for your dog as well as the foundation of positive reinforcement training. We'll also be looking at ways to set up a training schedule and build a bond with your pet, even if you're a busy person.

UNDERSTANDING YOUR DOG'S NEEDS

Dogs are living, breathing, and loving creatures, just like humans. They also have basic needs like food, water, shelter, exercise, hygiene and grooming. Years ago, dogs were often seen as work animals and were used in countless different scenarios in which they had a duty to perform.

Even though working dogs still play an important role in modern times, the big movement toward companionship has helped us understand their needs better. We now know that giving them the bare minimum will result in bare minimum performance, whether in a working environment or training.

If you think about it, we're much like dogs in this case. If we don't eat nutritious food, we're more likely to develop health problems. If we sleep uncomfortably, we'll be tired and grumpy the next day. If we don't get enough stimulating activities, we can even become depressed.

I like using this analogy because it helps us better understand that dogs are much more intricate animals than we give them credit for. It allows us to take on a new perspective and see the huge responsibility that we have toward them.

Food

When it comes to caring for our dogs, our first concern should always be their health and growth. Nutrition plays a crucial role in the health of your dog, especially as puppies. Puppies grow rapidly, and for them to avoid any developmental issues, they need the right kind of nutrition to keep them strong and happy. In Chapter 2, we will delve deeper into the topic of how to feed your dog.

Water

Giving your dog water might seem like an obvious thing, but there is a right and a wrong way to do it. Your pet should have access to clean, fresh water at all times. At the least, your dog's water bowl should be cleaned with soap daily. Replace their water in the morning and evening.

I personally don't believe in self-watering bowls, because it makes it hard to monitor how much water they've had for the day. To check for dehydration, pinch a bit of skin between your fingers at the shoulder, and if they're hydrated, it should spring right back when you release it. If they're dehydrated, the skin will take much longer to spring back.

Your dog's activity level, health, age, and type of food that they eat will have an impact on how much water they need. Dogs can become dehydrated in as little as a day, so it's very important to keep an eye on their water intake. If your dog stops drinking water or starts drinking water excessively, you should consult your veterinarian, as this may be an early sign of sickness or disease.

A Place to Sleep

Where your dog sleeps depends on an array of different factors, such as individual personality, comfort for both you and your dog, your preferences for spaces you want your dog in, and their age. The most important thing when it comes to your dog's bed is that they recognize it as a safe space and can get a comfortable night's sleep.

Think about what you would want in a bed—in cold weather, perhaps you would like an extra blanket or two. Something comfortable like a pillow, cushion, or mattress to lay on, and a space where you're protected from the elements.

While most dog owners I know prefer that their dogs sleep inside, there are cases where it is acceptable to let your dog sleep outside. If your dog is a working dog, for instance, a guard dog or livestock guard dog, they will likely do most of their work outside at night.

In this case, they should be provided with proper shelters like a dog house, a comfortable bed, and freshwater close by. As long as your dog feels safe and comfortable and can escape from any harsh climatic conditions, this is perfectly fine. However, there are risks associated with this. I wouldn't let my working dogs sleep outside before they're properly trained.

When choosing a spot for their resting place in your home, ensure that both you and your dog are comfortable with it. Ensure they can't get to anything dangerous during the night, like something they're not allowed to eat. We'll be looking at crate training in more detail in Chapter 4, but where you place the crate in your home will depend on your unique situation. Some dogs don't mind sleeping in a different room than you, while others feel safer and more comfortable sharing a room with their *pack*.

If you enjoy cuddling up to your best friend at night, no one can tell you that you're wrong. There is a common misconception that letting your dog sleep in your bed leads them to believe that they have dominance over you, and this is completely false and outdated. If you and your dog are comfortable, go for it. However, some dogs may benefit from learning to sleep in their crate if they require stricter boundaries. Very small puppies should be restricted to their crate in the evenings and kept in a place where you can keep your eye on them to avoid any accidents.

Exercise

Exercise is a massively important part of your dog's health, and all dogs need exercise at varying levels, depending on age, breed, stamina, and health condition. Not only does exercise stimulate their brains, but it also keeps them in shape. A lack of exercise can lead to poor health physically and mentally.

Different breeds typically have different energy levels, and therefore different exercise requirements. It's important to do thorough research on their breed to understand their needs better. Breeds with moderate energy levels need at least 30 minutes of exercise a day, whereas breeds with moderately high to high energy levels need between 60 and 120 minutes of exercise.

Toy- and small dog breeds generally need less exercise than larger breeds. They're fine with some play and moderate-paced walks for 30 minutes and shouldn't be subjected to too intense exercise.

Brachycephalic dogs are dogs with flat or very short noses, such as pugs, American bulldogs, bull mastiffs, Boston terriers, and boxers. Because of their short or flat noses, breathing may become a problem during intense exercise, which is why it's better to stick to moderate exercise for short periods of time. The amount of time they should be exercising in total will depend on the energy level of the breed.

Large and giant breeds are prone to joint problems, making joint-intense exercise a risk for them. Exercises like swimming, walks, and short fetch sessions will work well for them. Around 30 to 45 minutes of exercise should be sufficient for them. High-energy breeds like Collies and Huskies need a minimum of 60 to 120 minutes of exercise a day, with at least 60 minutes being intense exercise.

When choosing an exercise for your dog, keep their state of health in mind. For instance, if they're recovering from illness or something similar, it's better to let them focus their energy on recovery. If they have existing joint problems, you should move more towards low-intensity exercise.

Puppies should be introduced to exercise slowly. Just like us, they need time to build up stamina. Senior dogs will have a smaller need for exercise and their activity levels will slow down naturally.

Keep a close eye on your dog when they're exercising to ensure that they don't overheat or injure themselves. If they start drooling and panting excessively or their tongue and insides of their ears start turning bright red, this may be a sign of heat exhaustion.

Enriched Environment

Before we can provide our animals with an enriched environment, we need to have a thorough understanding of what it means. Enrichment refers to something that will satisfy their physical and psychological needs and stimulate them to be more active. It can also be something that encourages their natural behavior and curiosity (*Environmental Enrichment*, n.d.). Enrich your dog's environment with snack puzzles, toys, snuffle mats, and lick mats, which can encourage healthy play and good behavior.

Basic Supplies

Owning a dog comes with challenges, so let's avoid creating more challenges by not having the right supplies! Here is a list of the basic things that you will need to take care of your dog:

- Collar: A collar is important because it can help identify your dog and get them safely back to you in case they get lost or slip out somewhere. You might think that there is no way it could happen, but in my experience, never say never in this case. We should always be prepared for the unforeseen.
- Water and food bowls: Food and water bowls should be easy to clean and durable. For dogs that eat too fast, consider a slow feeder.
- Leash: You will need a leash to take your dog on walks and train them.
- Crate: The crate is used in crate training and doubles as a safe space for your dog.
- Bedding: Your dog will need comfortable bedding suited for the weather.

- Food storage container: You don't want their food getting stale, so sealing it in a food-safe container is a good idea.
- Food measuring scoop: Used to measure the exact amount of food that your dog needs per meal.
- Toys: Toys are used to enrich their environment and during playtime or training.
- High-value treats: Tasty treats are a great way to encourage good behavior and will help in training.
- Poop bags: When in public spaces, it's not only good manners to clean up after your dog but also usually mandatory.
- Grooming supplies: We'll be taking a look at what you need for grooming in the next section.

Grooming

Dogs need to be groomed regularly to stay on top of hygiene and make them more comfortable. Neglecting grooming in dogs can lead to skin problems and infections, painful and overgrown nails, matted coats, and inflammation.

Grooming includes the following:

- clipping nails every three to four weeks depending on how fast they grow
- daily thorough coat brushing

- bathing them somewhere between once a week and once a month depending on their breed
- brushing their teeth up to once a day
- trimming hair that causes inconvenience or dirt buildup
- Gently cleaning the ears when there is a lot of wax buildup

Nail clipping can be a very nerve-wracking experience if you're new to it. Cutting their nails too short can lead to bleeding and pain for your pet, and we really want to avoid this when possible. If your pet regularly walks or plays on hard surfaces like concrete, their nails can become naturally filed down.

However, this is not always the case, and keeping their nails trimmed will enable them to move around more comfortably. Start trimming your dog's nails as a puppy and be sure to give them a treat and a lot of praise to encourage them to allow it. Only trim off a tiny bit of the nails at a time to avoid injuring your pet.

It's recommended to take your dog to a professional groomer at least every three months to keep them in good shape. Daily care and maintenance are still very necessary. When bathing your dog, only use veterinary-approved dog shampoos. Other products can cause irritation or damage to the skin.

Most people would have never guessed it, but yes, you have to brush your dog's teeth! It's important to use a dog toothbrush and toothpaste, as regular toothpaste is not made to be ingested and can cause stomach problems.

When trimming your dog's hair, focus on trimming around the eyes and behind-area. You can also trim excessive hair under the paw pads. You don't have to do a perfect job the first time around, and it might take a few tries to make it look perfect. Your puppy should be groomed from around 10 weeks old but avoid bathing them in cold weather. Grooming them from a young age and giving them praise and treats while doing so will help make the experience more enjoyable for you and them. Always dry them thoroughly after bathing and check for ticks and fleas.

When cleaning your dog's ears, avoid cleaning too deep. The ears are sensitive organs and shouldn't be cleaned unless there is actually wax and dirt buildup. You can use a soft cloth with lukewarm water or ear wipes that can be bought from a vet shop.

The basic grooming kit includes the following:

- a brush specific to the type of coat that your dog has
- dog nail clippers
- ear cleaning wipes or cloth
- veterinarian-approved dog shampoo

- dog toothbrush and veterinarian-approved toothpaste
- trimming scissors or an electric trimmer

THE SCIENCE OF POSITIVE REINFORCEMENT

Now that we know exactly what our dogs need to live a happy, healthy life, we can start looking at training. It's important that we focus on their health and well-being first, but once we've done that, effective training becomes one of the crucial tools in building a trusting relationship with your pet.

How is positive reinforcement training different from conventional, dominance, and punishment-based training? Punishment-based training focuses on negative reinforcement, which means punishment immediately after a bad behavior. Punishment will involve some form of causing discomfort for the dog, like spraying them with water, spanking, yelling, shock collars, and more.

The idea behind negative reinforcement training is to try to make the dog understand that you're the alpha and have the dominance. They need to obey your wishes, or else. This kind of training aims to make the dog associate the discomfort with the bad behavior, therefore not repeating it. In reality, it actually does the opposite.

Dominance training causes fear, anxiety, confusion, and distrust in your dog. Sooner or later, your dog may start to associate you with that feeling of discomfort rather than the bad behavior. This kind of training causes so much more harm than good and can actually encourage your dog to behave badly.

Let me explain—dogs see attention as a reward. Some dogs may not even distinguish between good and bad attention and will act out for any attention at all. They start to learn that if they continue their bad behavior, they get your attention. Of course, this is something that we want to avoid. Therefore, the first principle of positive reinforcement training is not to reward bad behavior in any way, especially by giving them attention.

When the dog is doing something that you don't want them to do, positive reinforcement training teaches you to ignore them. No eye contact, no acknowledgment. This shows them that if they exhibit this behavior, they won't be getting any attention from you. The moment they stop the bad behavior and exhibit the behavior that you want them to, you reward them.

Always rewarding good behavior is considered to be the second principle in positive reinforcement training, and also the most important part. Your dog should be rewarded for good behavior within seconds of the action to affirm that they're doing something right. They will start associating the good behavior with reward, causing them to repeat it willingly.

This leads me to the third principle—no punishment. This may sound absurd at first, but there is a very good reason for this that has to do with how a dog's brain works. Dogs can become insensitive to punishments after a while, making them ineffective in any case. Their brains place rewards higher up on the priority list than punishment, meaning that rewards have a longer-lasting effect on their behavior than punishment.

Conventional punishment-based training can become cruel and inhumane. Things like anti-bark collars and spanking can cause your pet to become fearful and anxious. The problem with this kind of training is that most of the time, the dog may feel confused about what you want them to do, whereas positive reinforcement training teaches them exactly what the right actions are.

Positive reinforcement training isn't only about getting your dog to do what you want them to but also about understanding them better. You will learn to read their body language which can help you identify ways to improve your training structure daily. Just like with us, all dogs have unique personalities.

Rewarding

When it comes to rewards, there are a few options that we can use:

- Attention: Acknowledging your dog, speaking to them, and physical touches like pets or ear scratches.
- Praise: Using praise like "good boy" in a friendly tone of voice shows your dog that you're happy with what they're doing.
- Treats: In most cases, treats are the highest-valued rewards.
- Playtime: Playing fetch or tug war with your pet is a great way to reward them for good behavior.
- Toys: Giving them their favorite toy encourages them to repeat the wanted behavior.

Even though treats are mostly the favorite among rewards for dogs, your dog may have a different preference depending on their personality. Treats are a great way to give them an immediate reward, but you can't give them a treat every single time forever. This is why it's good to alternate between rewards.

Isn't it a good feeling to know that your dog will do what you want them to willingly, instead of being forced by fear and anxiety? They will behave well because they will consider it fun and pleasing to you. This is what we want to build with the right kind of training—a happy dog that understands you and what you expect from them. If they know what you expect from them, it's just so much easier to reinforce good behavior.

THE IMPORTANCE OF CONSISTENCY

Habits, whether good or bad, are formed by repeating actions over and over again. The neuropathways in the brain change and make new pathways for specific action. Therefore, we should be mindful of the actions that we repeat, as well as the behavior that we allow from our pets. It's much harder to break a habit than to learn a new one.

In positive reinforcement training, consistency is key to success. If you think about it, it's quite obvious why. If we continuously reinforce good behavior, there is no confusion for our dogs about what we expect from them. However, inconsistency can lead to confusion and hinder the formation of good habits, even promoting the formation of bad habits in some cases.

Stay consistent with things that you deem acceptable and things that you don't when training your dog. For instance, if you allow them on the furniture one day and don't want them to get on the next, you're confusing them. Set some house and behavioral rules and stick to them.

Establishing a routine with your pet, including set training and feeding times, can lead to better behavior and consistency in their life. When they have a routine, controlling their behavior is much easier. For instance, if pets are fed at consistent times, they are less likely to beg.

When choosing words for commands, keep them simple and short, and stick to them. Don't choose more than one word for a command. Ensure that everyone in your household is on the same page with command words and your method of training overall, or your training might become ineffective. As an example, if your rule is no begging for food, but your partner feeds the dog from the table, it's completely counterproductive. Remember to always reward good behavior, even if it's just with words of praise. Consistently rewarding leads to consistent behavior.

BUILDING TRUST AND A STRONG BOND

Trust is the most important thing in any relationship. If you don't have trust, you have nothing. Let's put ourselves in our dog's shoes. If you feel distrust toward someone, how likely are you to cooperate with them?

The bond between a dog and their owner knows no limits. They have the capability to build bonds with us that can easily overshadow our bonds with some people. We have the incredible honor of taking care of these amazing creatures and learning what true love is through their companionship, and we should thank them by doing everything we can to build a strong bond.

A strong bond is an unnegotiable requirement in any dog training. The lack of a bond will cause training to be slow and unproductive. Having a bond with your dog makes them feel safe, comfortable, and happy around you. They will be more likely to follow commands and cooperate during training.

Dogs that have a strong bond with their humans often don't react as badly to new and scary situations as dogs that don't. This is because they feel safe with you and know that you're by their side to protect them. If your dog trusts you, they will brave situations that may have caused fear and anxiety if they didn't.

When it comes to building a bond, all dogs are different. The important thing is that you allow them to move according to their pace. You should never try to force your dog to do an activity if they're not ready. This can easily break trust. Instead, learn to recognize their cues in body language and behavior.

If your dog seems uninterested in training or treats, it's a good indication that they're overstimulated or tired. Instead of pushing them past their limits, give them some time to relax. Your dog's body language will differ from that of other dogs. For instance, when my dog is excited, he curls his lip and wags his tail. Lip curling is usually associated with aggression and fear, but because I spend a lot of time with my pet, I've learned that this is merely a way of telling me that he's excited.

Dogs can't talk and will communicate with their bodies. The best way to get to know your dog and understand what they're communicating to you is by watching them and making mental notes on their behavior. Even though there are some standard behaviors that are generally relevant to most dogs, you should get to know your dog personally to understand them.

A dog's trust may seem never-ending, but they do have limits. If you disappoint them often, it can damage your relationship with them. Spend quality time with your dog other than training to build a stronger bond. Respect their space and boundaries, and they will respect yours.

A good indication that you have a strong bond with your dog is if they seem relaxed and comfortable around you. They will approach you and ask for attention, and they may wag their tail and seem excited. A dog that doesn't trust you completely may seem tense, tail straight or between the legs, and won't approach you.

The most valuable thing that you can give your dog to promote a healthy relationship with them is your time. While many claim that there are textbook ways to bond with your dog, the truth is that there isn't. Because every dog is unique, every bonding experience will be unique. However, spending time with them and giving them affection while respecting their boundaries is the most basic way that you can build a good bond with them.

Building a bond may take time. Always be patient and willing to put in the work, and they will reward you with their loyalty tenfold. Don't make your expectations unrealistic. Some dog breeds are predisposed to fear and anxiety and will take longer to warm up to you. In other cases, an adopted dog that has a history of abuse or trauma can take even longer. The key here is patience and persistence. Show them that humans are capable of loving and trusting.

SETTING UP A TRAINING SCHEDULE

Having a training schedule will make it easier to train your dog successfully. Whether your day is packed, or you have some time to spare, an effective training schedule is a must. You might feel like you don't have the time to fit everything in, but there are ways in which we can set up our training schedules without taking away from our daily responsibilities.

The first step is to write down your own daily schedule. This will help you spot time in your day that you can dedicate to your dog. Your dog's training schedule should align effortlessly with your own to make it easier to manage.

Here are the things that should be incorporated into your training schedule:

- potty times
- playtime or exercise
- sleep or crate time
- training time
- meal time

Dogs are more likely to go potty after they've been active, so try to schedule potty breaks after walks or exercise. This is a great way to get them to form a routine and avoid unwanted accidents.

Work out the amount of exercise that your dog needs on a daily basis and break it up into smaller sections. You don't want to overwhelm your dog with all of their intense exercises at once and keep in mind that it should be a fun activity for both of you. Train your pup to sleep at the same time you do for more convenience. After they've had their play, exercise, and potty times, you can also incorporate some crate time for rest.

Although setting up training times in specific parts of the day is the most beneficial way to do it, very busy individuals might not have as much time to do so. Training can take place throughout any activity during the day, for instance, meal times. You can train your dog to do a few commands before mealtime, and they're rewarded with their tasty meal. Try to incorporate some training during play and exercise time as well, which will help you save some time.

Training sessions should be short and fun for both of you. You don't want your dog to become bored and demotivated by pushing them through rigorous and long training sessions at a time. Dogs train better in short five to ten-minute training sessions in any case. Your dog loves spending time with you and will often mimic your behavior. Training them to have mealtimes at the same time you do will also create an opportunity for bonding.

Put your written training schedule somewhere where everyone in the household can see it, and make sure that everyone is on board. If something comes up and you can't fulfill part of the schedule, or if you go on a trip and get someone to look after your dog, it's important that they will be able to stay consistent with the schedule in your absence.

Create some realistic training goals for your dog to ensure that you keep an eye on what you want to accomplish and adjust your training accordingly. Keep their physical ability, age, personality, breed, and all other factors that might contribute in mind when doing so. Your dog won't be a fully trained dog after one week, and patience is key. Go according to their pace, and the results will be astounding.

Example of a Training Schedule for a Busy Individual

The following table has an example of a training schedule for a working individual. Keep in mind that everyone's schedule will look different, and yours won't be the same as this one. This just serves as a way to show that training can be done even if you're a busy person. You will most likely have to adjust your schedule a few times to find the perfect fit for you.

Time	Action
07:00—07:30	Walk and leash training, potty time
07:30—08:00	Breakfast, two to five-minute training session with meal, rest
08:00—08:40	Get ready for work
08:40—09:00	Go to work
13:00—14:00	Go home for lunch, potty time, lunch, two to five-minute training session with a meal, go back to work
14:00—17:00	Work, go home.
17:00—17:30	Get dressed in active clothing (or anything that you prefer to walk in over your work apparel)
17:30—18:30	Walk and leash training, potty time, five-minute training session
18:30—19:30	Rest, grooming, take a shower
19:30—20:30	Dinner, two to five-minute training session with meal
20:30	Potty time, get ready for bed

2

THE ART OF FEEDING

> *Money can buy you a fine dog, but only love can make him wag his tail.*

— KINKY FRIEDMAN

F eeding your dog is a little bit more complicated than we may think. It can feel quite overwhelming to choose the right food for your pet when looking at the countless different options. If you think about babies, you know that they start off by drinking milk, then some softer foods, and then the harder stuff. Dogs have similar needs, with a few extra factors that play a role. The food that your dog needs as well as their feeding intervals will depend on their age, breed, reproductive stage, activity level, and health condition.

ESSENTIAL NUTRIENTS

Dogs need adequate amounts of the following nutrients in their diet:

Nutrient	Role
Carbohydrates	Carbohydrates are mainly used for energy in a dog's diet. Fiber is also a carbohydrate, and it improves gastrointestinal health by ensuring a healthy gut biome and also contributing to fecal bulk. Dogs with high energy needs will generally be fed a diet higher in carbohydrates.
Protein	Proteins are the building blocks of the body. It's used to build muscle, ligaments, teeth, bone, air, and cartilage. It also plays an important role in the production and management of hormones. Proteins are made up of amino acids. Specific amino acids are needed for specific functions in the body. Thus, proteins that don't contain the correct amino acids cannot fulfill their functions effectively. Animal-based proteins provide more essential amino acids for dogs than plant-based proteins.
Vitamins	Vitamins play countless crucial roles in the body. They're essential for immunity, brain function, metabolism, growth, and so much more. A balanced diet will contain all of the essential vitamins needed for a healthy body, whereas an unbalanced diet can lead to vitamin deficiencies and health problems.
Minerals	Minerals are inorganic compounds that contribute to everyday essential bodily functions of your pet. They play a role in healthy brain and nerve function, bones and teeth, hydration, and neuromuscular function.
Fats	Fats are great sources of energy for dogs and also play an important role in protecting organs, brain function, immune response, absorption of fat-soluble vitamins, and insulation. Fats are also needed to keep the skin and coat healthy. Omega 6 fatty acids are essential for growth, reproduction, and skin and coat health, while omega 3 fatty acids improve brain development and play a role in inflammation management.

FACTORS THAT PLAY A ROLE IN WHAT YOU FEED YOUR DOG

Age

Dogs can be categorized into three main life stages that have different nutrient requirements—puppy, adult, and senior. Dogs are considered puppies until one year of age, adults between one and five to ten years of age depending on the breed size, and seniors between five to ten years upwards. Small breeds will become seniors after the age of seven to ten, medium breeds are seniors at the age of seven, and large and giant breeds are considered seniors after five to seven years old.

Puppies grow rapidly, which means that they need nutrient-dense food. Puppy food will generally be higher in protein for healthy muscle growth and development, as well as fats for brain development and carbohydrates for energy. Small-breed puppy food contains higher levels of calcium, whereas large-breed puppy food contains much less. Large breeds can be prone to skeletal and joint problems when they're older, and if their bones grow too fast in the puppy stage, it will cause problems later in life.

Everything that we feed our dogs as puppies will have an impact on their health condition when they're older. This is why we should never feed large-breed puppies food with high calcium levels. Dogs are fed puppy food until the age of one year old. However, some larger breeds will have to be fed puppy food up to 18 months old. Thus, feeding your puppy high-quality and nutrient-dense food will significantly improve their quality of life now and when they're older.

When puppies are three to four weeks old, soft puppy food and water can be introduced. They need to be fed at least 4 times a day, and by six to eight weeks, you can move to dry puppy food. Reduce feeding intervals to three times a day by three months old, and by six months, they can be fed twice a day.

As our dogs move to adulthood, their growth will slow down, and they will require less nutrient-dense food. We call this stage *maintenance feeding.* As their bodies are no longer focusing on growth but rather maintenance of daily bodily functions, they will need less energy and calories in their diet. Adult dog food generally contains fewer proteins and fats. Feeding adult dogs puppy food can lead to massive weight gain and eventually to obesity, which brings an array of other health problems into the mix.

When our dogs become seniors, just like us, their activity levels drop exponentially. Less activity means that they need fewer calories to support their bodies. Weight gain is a common problem with senior dogs, as they don't get in as much exercise as they used to. This is why most senior dog foods contain fewer calories and more fiber. You will also find that many of them contain ingredients such as glucosamine, which aids in joint pain and arthritis management.

Unless your senior dog has a problem with weight management or joint pain, it's not paramount that you feed them senior dog food. However, the added ingredients that contribute to joint health can be a precaution. There are supplements that you can add to normal adult dog food for this, and whether you decide to feed your dog senior food or not will depend on their individual condition.

Breed

As we know, there are different sizes of dog breeds—small breeds, medium breeds, large breeds, and giant breeds. The breed size is determined by looking at the average weight of the dog in adulthood. Small breeds weigh 22 lbs. or less, medium breeds range between 22 and 55 lbs., large breeds range between 55 and 100 lbs., and giant breeds can weigh upward of 100 lbs.

Small dogs have fast metabolisms compared to medium and large breeds, which means that they require more energy in their food for maintenance. The other difference in breed size-specific dog food is the kibble size. Smaller breeds will need smaller kibbles to make it easier to eat, while medium and larger breeds will be able to eat larger kibbles.

As some breeds are more susceptible to certain health conditions, adding specific ingredients to their food as a precaution can be beneficial. There are several high-quality dog food brands available, including Royal Canin, which offers breed-specific dog food for this reason. It's not necessary to feed your dog breed-specific food, but it is important to feed them food specific to their size.

Reproductive Stage

Your dog should be fed a high-quality, balanced diet at all stages of life, whether they're reproducing or not. However, this is especially important when breeding. Any nutrient-related problems may lead to unsuccessful conception, pregnancy, or birth. If your dog is obese or underweight for instance, it will cause various problems and difficulty in reproduction.

The gestation period in dogs is about 9 weeks, or more precisely, 62 days. It may or may not be a day or two longer or shorter. During the first 6 weeks, a pregnant dog can eat normal adult dog food that is suited for her. It's important to keep an eye on their weight, as obesity can lead to complications. They shouldn't gain more than 20% of their body weight. They shouldn't lose any weight, and if they do, you can increase their food portion accordingly.

During the last few weeks of pregnancy, the dog will need nutrient-dense food with extra calcium. This aids in healthy fetal and milk development in the last stages, as the fetuses will grow fast during this time. You can feed them small or medium-breed puppy food depending on their kibble size preference, but never large-breed puppy food, which can lead to a calcium deficiency and abnormal fetal development. Even large-breed mothers should be fed small or medium-breed puppy food. You can continue to feed the puppy food until all of the puppies are completely weaned.

Activity Level

Working dogs and highly active dogs have a higher energy requirement than dogs that have a moderate level of activity. If your dog is busy with high-intensity training, they will also need additional energy sources.

Food specifically formulated for working and active dogs contains more proteins and fats, as their daily caloric intake can be up to three times as much as a moderately active dog depending on what they do. In this case, monitoring your dog's weight is essential to knowing whether you're feeding them enough.

Health Condition

Dogs, like humans, may require a specific diet for certain health conditions. There are high-quality prescription dog foods on the market such as Hills Prescription Diets. These foods will normally be recommended by a veterinarian.

Here are a few examples of health conditions that will require a specific diet:

Health Condition	Diet Requirement
diabetes mellitus	Diabetic dogs require foods high in fiber that are digested slower in order to control blood sugar levels.
pancreatitis	Patients with pancreatitis require a low-fat, digestible diet. However, pancreatitis may present differently in individual cases, and you will need to consult a veterinarian on your dog's diet.
arthritis	Arthritic dogs will benefit from food that contains added omega-3 fatty acids, chondroitin sulfate, and glucosamine.

When feeding specific diets to alleviate health conditions, it's incredibly important to consult your veterinarian. With conditions such as pancreatitis, you can do more harm than good by feeding the wrong diet. It's also important that you don't self-diagnose. It's better to obtain a correct diagnosis for your dog's health instead of risking worsening the condition.

Dogs that are malnourished or sick may need more calories and nutrients than healthy dogs. In this case, you can feed them puppy food until they have recovered, but they shouldn't stay on it for too long.

Dry vs Wet Food

We all want to see our pets happy, and it's no secret that dogs enjoy wet food much more than dry food. However, in order to keep their teeth and gums healthy, dogs should always be fed dry food when possible. Dry food helps scrape the teeth clean while the dog eats, while wet food can lead to tartar buildup and eventually deterioration of gum and tooth health.

Wet food can be given as a treat once in a while, but refrain from giving it daily. The amount of wet food you give as a treat should also be included in the daily calorie count that your dog needs. The amount of food that your dog needs daily will be indicated on the packaging of the dog food but should also be adjusted in case of the scenarios mentioned above.

THE ROLE OF FOOD IN TRAINING

Food is an important part of the reward system in positive reinforcement training. Because most dogs are highly food-motivated, it's the fastest way to reward them and get them to show the wanted behavior. Remember that all dogs have unique personalities, which means that they have unique preferences when it comes to food.

Some dogs aren't as food-motivated as others and may respond better to things like praise and physical affection. However, if your dog isn't showing interest in the treats you're offering during training, it might just not be their preferred snack!

There are countless healthy snack options on the market and at home that you can offer your dog. They're bound to like at least a few of the many options. Changing up their treats regularly will ensure that they don't get tired of the same treats and lose interest, and it will also allow you to learn about their preferences.

Food supplies all of the nutrients that your dog needs to be able to function, learn, and be active. If their diet isn't right, they'll have a hard time with training. As we've seen in the previous section, food plays a massive role in the health of your pup. An unhealthy dog will be less willing to learn and struggle with focusing on training sessions. A lack of quality food may lead to underdevelopment, fatigue, and other health problems. Overall, food plays a pivotal role in training in regard to rewards and health.

TIMING YOUR DOG'S MEALS

Timing your dog's meals creates security for your pet. Dogs are habitual animals and find comfort in knowing that they will be fed at a specific time. Think about it—if you were a dog, wouldn't you feel less anxious if you were fed at the same time every day? A feeding schedule also prevents unwanted behaviors such as begging.

A feeding schedule is not only better for our dogs but also for us. If you feed your dog at different times every day, it can be easy to forget to feed them or forget whether you've fed them already. Our dogs should have balanced meals in the right amounts every day at the same time to avoid obesity, underfeeding, and stress.

Self-feeders are not recommended and with good reason. With a self-feeder, there is no sure way to know how much your dog ate, or whether they ate at all. One of the first things that we see in sick dogs is the lack of appetite.

When dogs are feeling unwell, they will eat less or stop eating overall. This is your first red flag. If you don't know how much your dog is eating, there are cases where there is no other way to tell that they're sick until it's too late. By the time other symptoms start showing, the illness has already progressed, and you can expect to pay a hefty bill at the vet. If you notice a lack of appetite and catch an illness early on, chances are your dog will recover faster and need much less treatment.

Letting your dog eat whenever they want can cause obesity, which as mentioned above, causes numerous other health complications. If left to their own devices, most dogs are guaranteed to overeat. Quality dog food isn't cheap, and if they're eating more than they require per day, you could end up paying double for dog food than you would have if they ate the right amount. A meal schedule also allows you to incorporate training into meal times.

Puppies will eat around four times a day until they're four months old, three times a day until they're six months old, and twice a day from then on forward. The total amount of food that they need a day should be divided by the amount of times that they're fed to give you the correct amount to feed per meal.

CHOOSING THE RIGHT TREATS

When choosing treats, keep the calorie count in mind. Excessive high-calorie treats can cause your dog to become overweight, which we want to avoid. Look for low-calorie, healthy treats at your local vet store. You can also give them healthy treats from the fridge:

- cooked chicken meat cut into small pieces. Don't use any salt or seasoning. This is a very high-value treat.
- carrots
- watermelon
- blueberries
- apple slices
- cucumber slices
- strawberries

Even though we might be tempted to give our dogs some of our food from our plates, this is an absolute no-no. Dogs aren't made to eat as much salt as we do, which is the first problem. Our food contains way too much salt and oils, which can be damaging to your dog's health.

Treats should make up less than 10% of your dog's overall diet in calories, and anything more than that can also be damaging to their health (*Choosing the Right Dog Treats for Your Pooch*, n.d.). Avoid giving your dog treats that are high in preservatives, artificial coloring, and other unhealthy chemicals.

Always check the label for the source and quality of ingredients. This will give you a better idea of how healthy the snack is for your dog. Fewer ingredients in treats are always better because it's less likely to give your dog an allergic reaction or stomach problems.

It's important not to overdo it with any treats, and alternate between them so that your dog doesn't become too used to them. Treats should always be in the form of small pieces. You can start out training relying on food as a reward but wean them off of the treats as rewards little by little.

A good way to do this is by starting out with a treat every time your dog does a command. The next week, you can give them a treat every four out of five times or so, giving them another form of reward once. The week after that, you can try giving them a treat every three out of five times. Try to make it as unpredictable as possible. Sooner or later, they won't even need treats to do a command, and you can give them a treat every now and then.

AVOIDING OVERFEEDING

Obesity is one of the leading causes of health problems in dogs, and overfeeding is to blame. When we want to show affection, we often offer food to our pets. This isn't a bad thing but overdoing it will cause much more harm than good.

Eliminate table scraps from your pets' diet entirely. Not only is it unhealthy because of the high salt and oil content, but it's usually also high in calories. You might think that a few bites don't make a difference, but all of those calories add up and cause overfeeding at the end of the day. It is important to ensure that every member of your household is aware of the rule that prohibits giving table scraps to pets.

Everything that goes into your dog's mouth should be added to their daily calorie count, including treats. This is another reason why the treats you choose should be healthy and low in calories. To sum it up—stick to the recommended amount of food for your dog, follow a consistent meal schedule, avoid giving any additional treats, and opt for low-calorie options.

FOOD-RELATED BEHAVIORS

Begging

Having a dog that begs for food is not only inconvenient but can also put you into some embarrassing situations. You don't want your dog to beg for food when you have guests over, making them feel uncomfortable.

Why do dogs beg for food in the first place? The common misconception is that dogs beg because they're hungry. When humans domesticated dogs, the main attraction was food. Dogs are natural scavengers and therefore overate when food is available in case they have to go long times without it.

Your dog may beg for food due to a primal instinct to find food whenever they can. Even though it sounds strange, they may even beg for food after being fed due to this reason. The other reason they beg is because they just love food! The smell of food can be very enticing, and they will try to get a bite whenever possible.

To stop your dog from begging, feed them at the same time you have your meals whenever possible. This can keep them occupied while you have your meal. Ensure that they're fed in a separate room or keep them away from the dinner table when you're eating. You can train them to go to their crate after they've finished their meal with a command. Ignore any begging behavior to discourage them from keeping at it.

It's important that you keep a strict rule about begging behavior because they learn this very fast. Don't give in to their puppy dog eyes, and make sure that everyone in the household follows your lead.

Counter-Surfing

To many owners, counter-surfing is a major problem. This refers to when your dog steals food from tabletops or counters by jumping on the table or grabbing something from the side. As you can imagine, this is very bad behavior and should be addressed.

Dogs counter-surf to find food and snacks. They are rewarded when they get what they're looking for and therefore continue this behavior. The simplest way to stop them from doing this is to remove all forms of food from the counter so that they're not rewarded.

There are times when this is a bit impractical, so we turn to preventative training. Train your dog to go to their crate while you're working with food in the kitchen. Reward them for that, and they will continue the right behavior. Dogs may counter-surf out of boredom and lack of stimulation, so ensure that you have a stimulating environment and play times during the day to prevent this.

3

MASTERING POTTY TRAINING

> *The love of a dog is a pure thing. He gives you a trust which is total. You must not betray it.*
>
> — MICHEL HOUELLEBECQ

THE IMPORTANCE OF POTTY TRAINING

There are a few reasons why potty training is crucial for a dog owner, with the most obvious being that we don't want to deal with the mess in our homes. Potty training can help you avoid embarrassing situations at home or in public spaces. If your dog is trained to go at specific times or places, you're less likely to have an unfortunate event.

A dog that is potty trained is a dog that is not confused. Ensuring that your dog knows when and where to go can reduce their anxiety. Any training can be a bonding experience, even potty training. This can help strengthen your relationship with your dog.

Just like my mother was upset about her new carpet being ruined, it's natural for you and others in your household to become upset about accidents. You're likely to have a closer bond with your dog and won't be upset for too long, but someone in your household might develop a dislike for your pup. This is something that we want to avoid because you want everyone in your family to be at peace with your pet. Potty training can help prevent this and strengthen the bond between your dog and others in the household.

SETTING A POTTY SCHEDULE

Dogs need to go potty more or less frequently depending on their age. Puppies have small bladders and will need more frequent potty breaks, while older dogs don't need as many. Your potty schedule should be customized to your dog's age to prevent accidents.

Very young puppies may need potty breaks as frequently as every one to two hours. As they grow and their bladder control improves, they will need less frequent potty breaks. Fully grown dogs will need to go potty three to five times a day, depending on their activities. If you take your dog outside frequently for bathroom breaks, you'll have fewer or no accidents to deal with.

As we've discussed in Chapter 2, we can expect your dog to want to relieve themselves after certain activities like playtime, walks, and meals. Because we have this information, we can more or less predict when a good time would be to take them to the potty spot. Potty times should be directly after these activities. It won't take more than five minutes to take your dog outside for a potty, so you can easily fit it into your schedule.

Some dogs will show specific behaviors when it's time for them to go and learn how to signal it to you. For instance, they will bark at the door. In smaller puppies, watch their behavior before they go. Things like sniffing around can tell you that it's time to take them outside. Once potty training starts, you will learn to recognize your dog's unique signals.

When choosing somewhere that you want your dog to go regularly, always make sure that you go with them. As always, positive reinforcement training should be implemented in potty training. When they go potty in the right spot, make a big deal about it with praise or other rewards. This will help them form a habit of going to the right place.

CREATING A POTTY SPOT

When choosing a place for your dog to relieve themselves, be consistent about it. Dogs like to go to the same places and giving them multiple places to go may be confusing.

Go to the same spot in the yard and make sure that you clean up after them as soon as possible. If the spot isn't cleaned regularly, it may discourage them from wanting to use it and cause accidents in unwanted places.

Dogs learn at different paces, but they generally form habits quite fast. Not only does this mean that they will form a habit of going to the right place quickly, but they can also form a habit of going to the wrong place fast. That's why it's crucially important not to leave them without a potty break for too long.

While you're potty training your dog, it's important to limit the amount of space they have access to so you can keep an eye on them. This will also help you recognize signals of when they need to go. If you leave your untrained dog to roam in a large space, they might leave you a surprise somewhere for later.

The spot you choose should be easy to clean and distraction-free. If you don't have a yard, you can create your own potty spot with artificial grass on a platform, or by placing a pee pad where you want them to go. It should be big enough so that your dog feels comfortable going there and not cramped.

Placing pee pads inside your home isn't the ideal way to potty train, because it might lead to a habit of going inside. However, for very young puppies it's a good way to prevent accidents on the floor.

Dogs don't like going near their eating or sleeping places, so try to have the potty spot as far away as possible from that. If your dog is relieving themselves in their crate, it may be an indication that they don't see it as their safe space or den. The crate may also be too big for them. You can take steps to make them more comfortable in their crate or reduce the size of it to prevent this.

DIY Indoor Potty Spot

You can get creative when creating your indoor potty spot, and it doesn't have to be exactly like this one. Feel free to use materials that are available to you. Most materials that you will need will be available at stores like Walmart or the local dollar store.

You will need a tray of some sort. Anything with ridges on the edges to prevent messes will do. For small dogs, even an old tote lid or boot tray will work. You will also need some fake grass, and plastic tiles with slots. This will prevent the fake grass from sitting inside the mess after use.

Place the slotted tiles inside the boot tray, and the fake grass on top. Make sure that you clean it after every use to avoid bad smells in the home. For smaller puppies, you can get a pee pad holder or use a boot tray and place a pee pad inside.

There are great indoor potties available online, and if you want to spend a little bit more, you can buy one of them. Keep in mind that it should be big enough to accommodate your dog when they're fully grown.

HANDLING ACCIDENTS

Potty training is one of the first things that you will teach your dog. If you've had a few accidents to deal with like I did with Bear, you know just how frustrating it can be. Of course, we can't be mad at the dogs for accidents, because they rely on the correct training from us to know when and where they're supposed to go potty. Feelings of anger are natural when we come across an accident. However, we should never direct our anger toward our pets.

The first thing to do is to stay calm. You might startle your dog if you run up to them shouting *no,* or anything similar. Don't say anything and just pick them up quickly and move them to the right spot. This is also a learning experience for you as the owner because our first reaction is usually to give them a loud *no.*

If they finish in the right place, you can reward them with a treat or praise and physical affection. Make sure that you clean up thoroughly where they might have messed up in the house, because if they're able to smell anything there they will most likely want to go potty there again.

Many outdated potty training techniques involve rubbing your puppy's nose in their mess, shouting at them or even spanking them. This is very destructive and should never be done. This training technique will cause them to be afraid to go potty when you're around, leading to more surprise accidents.

POTTY TRAINING TIPS FOR BUSY FUR PARENTS

Life can get busy, and potty training can be hard when you have a lot of other things to focus on. To prevent our dogs from creating bad habits, we should stay on top of things even though we're busy. This may sound impossible, but there are ways to incorporate potty training into your busy schedule.

The first tip is to align your dog's schedule with your own. Your schedule takes priority, but we should always try to find those extra few minutes in the day to stick to their training. If you're working full time, try to come home during breaks if possible. This will allow you to spend time with your pup and their potty training.

If you can't, try to ensure that your dog has access to the dedicated potty area at all times. You may come across an accident when you come home if they're not fully trained, but you can follow the steps on handling the accident as explained in the previous section. Clean it up thoroughly and spend time on your dog's potty training when you are home. Use weekends and off days to reinforce good behavior, and they will eventually start doing it when they're alone too.

It might take a bit longer than it would've if you were home all the time, but don't be discouraged. With consistency and continued reward for the right behavior, they will come around. Dogs are intelligent creatures, and they want to make us happy, so they just need time to understand how to do that.

Another option is to get a dog walker. This isn't a must, but having someone come around to take your puppy out for some fresh air and a bathroom break can be very helpful for a busy individual during weekdays. If this is the route you choose, it's imperative that the dog walker is up to date with your dog's training techniques. If they apply different training than you, it may lead to confusion and bad behavior.

If you're away from home for a longer time, you can section off an area in the house for them. Place their crate, food, and water bowls in the area, as well as a pee pad or indoor potty area. Try to place the potty area as far away as possible from the bowls and the crate. Once again, this isn't ideal, but it will do as a temporary solution. It may take a longer time to train your puppy but be patient. Stay consistent and you will see results!

4

SUCCESSFUL CRATING

I think dogs are the most amazing creatures; they give unconditional love. For me, they are the role model for being alive.

— GILDA RADNER

Some may be hesitant to include crate training in their dog's upbringing because of the stigma that it's cruel and unfair to the dog. Forget everything you've heard about crates, and let's start on a clean slate with some facts. In my opinion, crate training is an absolute must for every dog owner, and in this chapter, we'll be looking at why.

BENEFITS OF CRATE TRAINING

Crates or dog kennels are enclosed spaces usually made from hard plastic or a wire structure. It will come with doors either only on one side or on both and should always be sturdy and durable.

The common misconception is that your dog is being punished when placed in a crate, where in reality it's supposed to be quite the opposite. If you punish your dog by sending them to their crate, you're doing it wrong. They shouldn't associate their crate with negativity, but rather with comfort and a feeling of safety.

The crate is a place for your dog to go when they're feeling stressed, unwell, or want to relax. The idea is for them to see it as their den. Dogs will look for a small, safe spot to claim as their territory in which they feel comfortable, and the crate is just the place to do that.

Crate training has many benefits, of which one is its aid in house training. As I've mentioned, dogs don't want to soil their sleeping spot. When you're potty training a puppy, you can use the crate to help them develop more control over their bladders and teach them that there are certain times when they should go potty. The crate shouldn't be used as a way to reduce potty breaks, but rather to encourage them to get into the habit of going at the right time. You should still always give them sufficient potty breaks.

Young puppies can be quite mischievous when left unsupervised, and there are times when we just can't keep an eye on them. The crate keeps them safe from harm and prevents them from learning bad behavior while you're busy with something else. We all know how fast a puppy can swallow things that they're not supposed to and having them go to the crate while unsupervised can prevent this.

Dogs want to be with us as often as they can, but they can become over-excited and overbearing at times. When there are many distractions and the environment is busy, crating your dog will keep them from injury or injuring others by jumping on them, and also keep them from getting under your feet.

The crate allows us to keep our dogs close to us while knowing that they're safe and not causing mischief. They will appreciate being in the house while still being allowed the safety, comfort, and privacy of their crate.

Things like family gatherings or a lot of strangers in your home can either make your dog over-excited or cause anxiety. If they have a safe place to retreat to, it can reduce their anxiety, because they see it as their own territory. It's important that your guests know this and respect their space in the crate.

When leaving your dog at home for a few hours, the crate offers them safety and security. You never know what they can get up to or where they can injure themselves if you're not there and leaving them outside might cause them to learn bad behaviors like digging or barking due to boredom.

Rescued dogs or very anxious dogs will benefit greatly from having their own personal space to retreat to. When they feel overstimulated, agitated, or anxious, the crate is their safe haven. It's important for you to also respect their space, and never pull them out of their crate by force. They should come out by themselves. This will reinforce the idea that it's their space and they can be comfortable.

Traveling with pets without a crate can become chaotic, especially if you have an anxious or high-energy dog breed. If your dog is crate trained, the stressful venture of traveling becomes much easier for them because they travel in their safe space. We want to include our dogs in all activities possible to enforce a strong relationship with them, and a crate will allow you to take them along on trips with ease. If you want to go out on your trip or visit somewhere that isn't dog friendly, the crate will make them feel safer in an unknown environment and reduce anxiety.

In the event of an emergency, a crate-trained dog is a safe dog. We never know when disaster will strike, and having a dog that is comfortable in their crate during stressful situations will allow you to evacuate them faster. There are so many cases where dogs get lost or injured during natural disasters. A crate is a quick way to get your dog and prevent them from running away due to fear.

Overall, crate training is beneficial for both the dog and the owner. We want to make our dogs a part of the family activities, and a crate allows us to do so without the stress of injury or learning bad behaviors.

CHOOSING THE RIGHT CRATE

Choosing the right crate is crucial to efficient crate training. If the crate is too large, they may go potty inside. If it's too small, it will make them feel uncomfortable. The material of the crate is also an important factor, as well as the space you have available in your home and what purposes you intend to use it for.

I would recommend getting a crate that will be big enough for your dog when they're fully grown. This may sound counterintuitive, but there are ways to make the space smaller for a puppy to discourage using it as a bathroom. You can place dividers in the crate, and some crates are expandable.

Your dog should be able to turn around, sit, stand, and lie down comfortably in their crate. Measure the tip of their nose to the base of their tail, and also the top of their head to the floor when sitting down. Add three to four inches to these measurements, and you have the perfect crate size. If your dog is still a puppy, go on the general measurements of their full-grown breed size.

The next consideration is whether you want a crate your dog can see through, or a crate that's entirely enclosed. This will depend on your dog. If you're buying a crate for a full-grown dog, think about their personality. Anxious dogs might prefer a closed crate for more privacy, while others would want to be able to look through their crate to see you.

Your crate should always have sufficient ventilation. It should be durable and easy to clean. You should also be able to comfortably fit your dog's bed or bedding inside, and still give them enough space to move around comfortably.

Your dog may want to try and escape from their crate when you're not around, and we should always keep this in mind. We don't want them to injure themselves trying to get out. The type of crate that you choose should be strong enough to keep them from chewing through if they're prone to chewing, but also made from material that won't injure them.

Steel cage crates are a great option in my opinion, because they're strong and can be used for travel in a car. They're usually collapsible, so if you have limited space in your home this will be a good fit. You can simply collapse the cage and put it away when not in use.

If your dog prefers a closed crate, you can throw some material over it to make it more private. For dogs that are prone to chewing, the steel crate is probably the best option. However, keep in mind that they might injure their teeth or claws if they rigorously try to escape from it. Ultimately, the crate that you choose will depend on your dog's unique needs and personality.

Wooden crates are a popular option because they look better than steel crates. They're sturdy and can easily fit in with your decor. The challenge with wooden crates is that they can be hard to move around and can rarely be used for travel. They're also the most expensive option.

Hard plastic crates are great for dogs that want more privacy. They're easy to clean, and their light weight makes them a great option for travel. They range from cheap to expensive, and there are several options available on the market. Most of the time they're not collapsible, so if you don't have a lot of space, they might pose a challenge.

For smaller breeds, fabric crates might be a good option. They're lightweight, but they can be a bit harder to clean. They're also not ideal for travel or dogs that are prone to chewing, so consider what you want to use the crate for. If you want to travel regularly, you might want to consider one of the other options.

Where you place your crate makes a big difference. Don't place it in an isolated area like the garage, as your dog may feel anxious when not close to you. Choose a relatively central location where you spend a lot of time in the house; alternatively, place one in their sleeping spot and one in the central location.

HOW TO CRATE TRAIN A DOG

Crate training may take some time depending on your dog's personality. Crate training them as early as possible is always a good idea. The earlier, the better. When crate training, it's important that your dog never feels forced, or they might start to see it as a punishment.

Your dog should always be happy to go into the crate. This is why it's important to use the crate when you're home as well as when you go away. If you only use it when you're leaving, your dog may associate it with that and become hesitant to go into their crate.

Always be gentle. Never force your dog into the crate, but rather lure them in with some tasty treats. Place some treats near the crate as well as inside. Let your dog have the treats at their own pace. If they don't want to get into the crate at first, that's okay. It might take a few more tries to get them comfortable enough to do so.

Always keep the crate door open during the first stages. Speak to them with a happy, gentle tone of voice during the training. Once they get into the crate, give them another treat and praise. Don't close the door just yet, and allow them to get comfortable in the crate.

Place two to three toys or chews inside the crate for them to play with, and switch it up every few days. Don't leave them unsupervised with anything that can be chewed to pieces and swallowed. Once your puppy is comfortable in the crate. You can gently close the door. Feed them treats through the crate and keep praising them.

If you stay consistent, you will notice that your dog will become more and more comfortable in their crate. At this stage, you can start walking into another room and leave them alone for a bit. Don't leave them in the crate for longer than five minutes at a time at first, and increase their crate time gradually as they get more comfortable.

Choose a command, such as the word *crate* or *bed* every time you do crate training to encourage them to associate the word with the action. When they go into the crate on command, praise them and give them a treat.

Crate training can be quick or take longer depending on your dog's unique personality. It can take up to six months to fully crate train your dog, and patience and consistency are key. Ensure that your dog isn't wearing a collar or anything else during crate time to avoid the strangulation hazard.

Don't leave your dog in a crate for longer than they can hold their bladders. Crate time should be an occasional thing during the day and not the norm. Your dog still needs outside time, as well as playtime, and exercise. If you're forgetful like me, set an alarm for yourself for when it's time for a potty break or when crate time is over.

Don't let your puppy out of the crate immediately if they start crying. This will encourage them to do it every time, and they will quickly learn that they can get what they want from doing this. Rather take it a few steps back with the training to make sure that they're comfortable in their crate.

AVOIDING OVERUSE OF THE CRATE

Overuse of the crate should be avoided at all costs. If the crate is used for long periods of time, your dog might begin to see it as a punishment, thus doing exactly the opposite of what we want it to do.

Overuse of the crate can lead to a lack of exercise and playtime. The crate should never be used as the norm, and only in certain situations as we've discussed. Your dog's age and personality will determine how long they can stay in the crate. The golden rule is that your dog, irrespective of their age, should never be left in the crate for longer than they can hold their bladders.

When possible, make sure to give your dog a potty break before crating them. Adult dogs can go about half a day in the crate if they were given sufficient potty time before-hand, and puppies can be crated significantly shorter. There is no definite rule when it comes to crate time, except that they shouldn't be left in it for too long. How long too long is will depend on your dog. Some dogs become anxious when being left in the crate for longer than a certain time, so in conjunction with their age and the time that they can hold their bladders, you should take this into account when working out their maximum crate time. The more you observe your dog's behavior, the more you will know.

It's important to note that even though your dog *can* hold it in the crate for a certain time, you shouldn't keep them in the crate for the maximum time. Overuse of the crate can lead to a lack of exercise and playtime. I know it can be challenging to find time for exercise and playtime with a busy schedule, but the moment we take on the responsibility of owning a pet, we make a promise that we will try our very best to take care of them as they deserve. Try to find time, use some of the time-saving techniques that we've discussed, and set an alarm to let them out in case you forget.

There will be times when you will be forced to leave your dog in the crate for longer than you would like for safety or other reasons, and that's okay. As long as it doesn't become the norm, they'll be fine.

Dogs can develop bladder infections, anxiety, and bad behaviors if left in the crate for too long. They might even become aggressive if you try to get them to go to their crate. In the long run, it's all about balance. Make sure that the crate is a fun place to be with treats and toys and spend a lot of time on crate training, and you won't be sorry. Overall, the crate is an extremely useful tool in training and safety for your dog if you use it right.

TRANSFORM LIVES WITH YOUR REVIEW

UNLEASH THE POWER OF POSITIVE REINFORCEMENT

"Kindness to animals makes the world a better place."

— UNKNOWN

 Ever wonder if a small act could make a big difference? It can, and I believe you're the key to unlocking that change. Let me explain how you can help someone you've never met but who needs guidance on a journey with their furry friend.

Are you ready to make a lasting impact on a fellow dog enthusiast, maybe someone less experienced but eager to strengthen their bond with their canine companion? Our mission is to make "Effective Positive Reinforcement for Dogs" accessible to every dog owner out there. We're reaching out to you because, well, most people do judge a book by its reviews.

Here's the ask: could you lend a hand to a struggling dog owner by leaving a review for this book?

Your review costs nothing and takes less than 60 seconds, but it could change another dog lover's life. Your words might help...

- ...one more family build a stronger connection with their four-legged friend.
- ...one more pup find understanding and reduce anxiety.
- ...one more household prevent accidents and foster a peaceful environment.

To leave your review, simply scan the QR code below:

By doing this, you're not just reviewing a book; you're contributing to a community of dog lovers helping each other out. You're making a difference in the lives of those you've never met, but who share the same passion for their pets.

Thank you for being part of this positive movement. Your support means the world to dog owners everywhere.

Sandra FELLERS

Your Dog's Best Friend

PS - Did you know? Sharing something valuable not only enriches the lives of others but makes you more valuable to them. If you believe this book will help another dog owner, pass it along—the more, the merrier in our community of happy dogs and their humans.

5

CONFIDENT LEASH TRAINING

A dog will teach you unconditional love. If you can have that in your life, things won't be too bad.

— ROBERT WAGNER

L eash training will make up a large part of your dog's training sessions for quite some time, and there is a good reason for that. In most public spaces, you'll find that the law requires us to keep our dogs on a leash. Also, having your dog on a leash keeps both of you safer, and can also help you avoid some undesired or embarrassing situations.

My worst experience with this situation happened when I was in my early twenties. I regularly took my dog for a walk around the block to get us both some much-needed exercise and blow off some steam. In the area where I lived, we had strict rules on having dogs on leashes, and everyone generally kept their dog on a leash anyway to avoid problems.

One early morning, as we went on our regular walk, I noticed a family of three coming in our direction with a medium-sized dog. It was difficult to determine if the dog was on a leash from that distance, but it appeared well-behaved since it calmly walked beside its owners. I decided to go to the opposite side of the road with my dog because I didn't know whether it would be reactive to my dog or not.

As we got closer and the other dog turned its attention toward us, it was already too late. Their dog ran straight at us, and my first reaction was to freeze. I was so scared at that moment and a horrifying picture played out in my head. As the dog got closer, I stomped my feet and yelled out, and it stopped in its tracks.

As their dog barked at us aggressively, the owners didn't seem too concerned with their dog's behavior. They took their time to walk over to us, and the man calmly told their dog to leave us while trying to pick them up. The lady kept telling me that their dog was friendly, but that was certainly not the case. After several failed attempts and amidst my loud shouts, the man finally managed to grab the dog and lift him up.

Even though we came out of the incident uninjured, it could've played out very differently. You should never find yourself causing unnecessary fear and anxiety for someone else because of your negligence. Always be alert when in public with your dog. Even if your dog is on a leash, someone else's may not be. Who knows what would've happened if my dog were not on a leash? It would've been extremely difficult to control the situation, and things could've gotten ugly.

THE IMPORTANCE OF LEASH TRAINING

While training your dog can be based on personal preference in most areas, leash training is an absolute must. In most cases with training, you decide which behaviors you want from your dog, but when it comes to public spaces, there are certain standards that we must adhere to.

A dog not trained to walk on a leash is a hazard for themselves, you, and others. The most important function of the leash is safety. Without a leash, your untrained pup can easily run into traffic, attack other dogs or people, and just cause havoc overall. Without leash training, it's impossible to take your dog to public spaces with you. You'll also have a hard time giving them their recommended daily exercise without being able to go for a walk.

We should always try to make our dogs part of family activities, and an uncontrolled dog can cause more problems than anything else. This will also cause your dog to have to be left alone at home when the family is out and about, which is not a good thing.

Dogs that are not leash-trained may feel trapped and anxious when on a leash. This can cause aggression or pulling. You can easily injure yourself or your dog if they pull on the leash because they're placing unnecessary strain on their trachea, neck, and body. You also run the risk of hurting your back and joints.

If you're struggling with an untrained dog, you're less likely to be willing to take them on walks. We can get frustrated with them and become reluctant to give them the exercise that they need. This can lead to damage in the relationship and training.

If your dog doesn't know what you expect of them while on the leash, they'll become frustrated and anxious. Set clear goals for yourself about what you want them to do while on the leash. Think about whether you want them to walk in front or beside you. These little details are all up to personal preference, but you should still know exactly what you want them to do, or you might end up confusing them with inconsistent training.

You don't want to be pulled off of your feet by a dog that feels trapped. Bad behavior from dogs, especially certain breeds, is frowned upon in public. If you have a power breed like a pit bull, it's even more important for them to behave well to break stereotypes. We want our dogs to form good relationships with others around us, not only our own family.

Leash training is the perfect bonding opportunity for you and your pup. Imagine having such a well-trained and behaved dog that you can literally take them anywhere without worry. This certainly doesn't come overnight, and you will have to spend a lot of time on leash training to reach this point, but it will be well worth it.

Think of the leash as a communication tool between you and your dog. Your dog should be trained not to strain on the leash to improve understanding and communication between you. In this case, you will know your dog is anxious the moment they strain their leash, and they will know that you sense danger when you strain the leash.

Where patience and consistency are crucial in all areas of training, it is even more so with leash training. Leash training doesn't only affect you at home, but also anyone that you come in contact with in public. You're not only leash-training your dog for yourself but also for others. Don't be one of those owners whose dogs are a pain to be around. It's not the dog's fault that they haven't been trained correctly, but it certainly makes you want to avoid them.

A well-leash trained dog will walk with you where you want them to and won't pull on the leash. They won't get distracted easily and will stick to their stance. They should be taught certain commands that we'll be taking a better look at later in this chapter to make walking on the leash easier and more convenient for both of you.

CHOOSING THE RIGHT LEASH AND COLLAR

Choosing a leash and collar for your dog may seem like an afterthought to some, but in reality, it can mean the difference between successful and unsuccessful training. The mistake that many dog owners make is buying a collar and a leash because it looks fashionable, rather than thinking of its functionality and role in the training process. It's easy to fall into that trap with all of the beautiful options on the market these days, but we should try to avoid this.

Another common mistake that we see regularly is owners buying certain types of collars or leashes without doing research first. They often don't know how these products work and either end up misusing them or failing to train their dog successfully.

The type of collar and leash that will work for your dog will depend on breed, energy level, size, and personality. It may seem like some dogs are born to walk on a leash and excel at leash training, while others struggle significantly to refrain from bad behavior on the leash. This may have something to do with the wrong collar or leash.

Breeds that generally have difficulty breathing like flat-faced breeds may feel trapped and anxious in a normal collar. The collar places pressure on the trachea, making it even harder for them to breathe. If this is the case, they will feel uncomfortable when walking with the collar and may begin resenting it.

With these dogs, walking them in a harness is a much better option. The pressure is taken from the neck and distributed over the body, making it easier for them to breathe. They will also be able to walk for longer distances without becoming tired.

Smaller dogs also benefit from being walked in harnesses instead of a collar. Toy- and small breeds have fragile necks and backs and walking them by collar may lead to injury in certain situations. A harness makes it much harder for your dog to slip out and escape, meaning that it's safer for them.

I'm a fan of the harness instead of the collar because it means more safety for your dog, and the chances of them injuring themselves during training are also smaller. You have more control, and when something unexpected happens, you can safely pull your dog away without hurting them.

The challenge with harnesses is that they may be too warm for hot summer days, and some designs don't include a place where you can attach an ID tag. A harness should always be removed between walks, and it should fit tight enough so your dog won't be able to unexpectedly escape, yet loose enough to be comfortable. Dogs with narrow heads that can easily slip out of collars will be trained more efficiently with a harness than a collar.

If you go on regular hikes and other outdoor adventures with your best bud, a harness with a handle on the back can help you assist them when they get stuck somewhere or need some help getting up a steep area. These harnesses are usually made with a lot of coverage over the dog's body, so the material should be breathable, yet durable.

Choke chains or collars have been used in dog training for many years. These destructive collars work by tightening around the dog's neck the moment they pull on their lead. In most cases, there is no limit to how tight the chain will go. The harder they pull, the tighter it gets.

For obvious reasons, choke chains are cruel and counter-intuitive for positive reinforcement training. Your dog can get seriously injured if they're frustrated or scared and can cause fatal injuries to themselves in the worst-case scenario. Prong collars or pinch collars usually have small protrusions on the inside of the collar that stick into the dog's neck when they pull on their leash. These types of collars are also cruel, and definitely not recommended.

While many old-school trainers swear by these, I'm here to tell you today that they're not effective and actually harmful in countless ways to your dog. From neck sprains to damaged salivary and thyroid glands, the list goes on and on.

Large breed and giant dogs are usually best trained with collars or front-clip harnesses. A front clip harness is a good option for a strong dog that is inclined to pull. It's important to make sure that the material of the collar is strong and durable and check it every now and then for wear and tear. Your leash should also be strong, and you can consider getting a chain leash for extra strength. A chain leash will also prevent your dog from chewing on it.

You should be able to fit two fingers between the collar and your dog's neck at all times to ensure that it's not too tight, but it should fit well enough to prevent them from pulling out their heads.

When it comes to choosing the right leash, there are a few things to keep in mind. A retractable leash is great for when you want to allow your dog some extra space to explore safely but isn't ideal for busy areas with high traffic. Shorter leashes are better for these environments.

The rule of thumb is that the closer your dog is to you, the more control you have and the safer they are. If your dog is quite anxious, they will feel safer when closer to you and a shorter leash will be perfect. Leashes that have adjustable lengths are great for all occasions and dogs, and I would recommend getting yourself one of those.

Leash training can commence when your dog is as young as ten weeks old. Your pup will still have a lot of growing to do at that stage, and they will outgrow their first collar or harness. They can grow surprisingly fast, and for effective training, it's important that their gear fit well from beginning to end.

You will have to adjust the tightness of their harnesses or collars regularly to keep up with their growth. Always be prompt with this, because not doing so can affect the quality of training. Always keep an eye on the state of their collar or harness, because if it's damaged, it can lead to unexpected accidents when out in public.

TEACHING BASIC LEASH COMMANDS

Leash training is an exciting adventure for both you and your dog. It may take patience and time, but once you start seeing their progress, you'll feel a sense of accomplishment that's hard to explain to someone else! Remember that leash training should be fun for both of you and should always be done in a positive spirit. Young puppies struggle to focus for too long, so it's important to keep your training short and exciting.

It's important to introduce a leash and harness or collar to your dog when they're young so that they can get used to it. We can start with some moderate leash training when they reach 10 weeks of age. Introduce the leash to your puppy slowly by placing it near them letting them smell and inspect them, and reward them for it.

You can start training indoors at first in a space that doesn't have too many distractions. Make sure that it's somewhere where they feel safe and comfortable. Once they've started warming up to the leash and collar, clip the leash into the collar and lure them into it with treats. Give them a lot of physical affection and praise, and always speak in a soft, warm tone.

Some dogs may be hesitant to put on their collar or leash at first but stay consistent and patient with them. If you keep rewarding them for it, they will eventually come around. Let them spend some time in the collar or harness and leash and use this time to play with them or do a fun activity together. This will enforce the idea that when the leash and harness come out, they're about to have a good time. Don't leave the leash and collar on them while they're unsupervised, and try not to keep it on for too long at a time.

Once they're comfortable with being in the harness or collar, you can start training them to stay by the side that you prefer. If you want your dog to walk on the left, keep your treats in the left hand and hold the leash with your right hand, or the other way around if you prefer the right side.

Use a command like *heel* to signal that you want them to move to your side. If you use this command and they come to you, reward them. You can practice this a few times. Now try taking a step forward. If they move with you, reward them again. This will take a few sessions to teach, but it's a good start.

Once your puppy has figured out that they're rewarded by staying at your side and moving to you, you can start slowly walking in different directions with them. Rewards are very important in this stage.

Teach your dog a command like *let's go,* or *go* to signal that you will start moving and they should move with you. Keep rewarding every time your dog does it right, and they will walk comfortably with you in no time.

The next stage is to move to an area with a few more distractions to deal with. If your dog turns their attention toward you instead of the distraction, reward them. You can move to walking outside once your dog has been taught these basics. Remember to walk with them in the yard before attempting to go into the street.

Dogs might be fearful of things like cars, other dogs, or even other people. Don't push them too hard if they're reluctant to go outside the yard. Take them a few steps out, and reward them when they turn their attention toward you. You can take them out a bit further every day until you're eventually able to walk them with ease.

Troubleshooting

Some dogs may struggle with specific behaviors while leash training, and it can vary from dog to dog. Let's look at a few common issues that you may experience with your pup, and how to fix them.

Pulling

Pulling on the leash is the most common issue that we experience with leash training. One reason that dogs pull on their leashes is out of frustration. If they feel frustrated by equipment that doesn't fit right, or if you constantly pull the leash too tight on your end, you might be encouraging them to pull you.

Your leash should be relatively relaxed when walking your dog to ensure efficient communication and prevent them from getting frustrated. Distractions can also be something that encourages them to pull on their leashes, and if this is the case, you can focus more on this portion of the training. If a distraction is present and you call your dog to heal, reward them when they follow your command. If they turn their attention to you, reward them so that they can understand that they should focus on what you're doing while walking.

You might not be rewarding your dog often enough if they keep pulling on their leash. Take your training a few steps back and start again by rewarding them when they're walking next to you. Stay consistent, and they will catch on eventually.

Another way to discourage pulling is to stop in your tracks once they start tugging on the leash. If they stop pulling and come to you, you can reward them. You can do this as many times as it takes to help them realize that pulling won't get them very far.

Chasing or Getting Distracted

It's in a dog's nature to want to chase. They can see things like squirrels and the instinct to catch prey immediately kicks in. In this case, the best way to unlearn this behavior is to go back to the basic recall training.

It may be necessary to spend some extra time training in environments that don't have many distractions and work your way up to more distracting areas. You can direct this chasing behavior in a positive way by playing fetch or something similar.

Chewing on the Leash

You might see the leash and collar as a walking aid, but your dog may see it as a toy. This is perfectly natural. Dogs are playful and curious by nature, which is why it's not surprising that they might want to play with their leash. However, cute as it may seem, this is a problem when trying to leash train your dog. To prevent this, try to give your dog another option to keep in their mouth, like a toy or a ball. You can also consider getting a chain leash to discourage them from chewing on it.

Taking the time to learn about your dog's personality traits and likes or dislikes can really aid in leash training. With all of the benefits of a well-leash-trained dog, why not take a shot at it? Even if your dog is older, with consistency and patience, you can do it! In the next chapter, we'll be going into detail about successfully house-training your pup.

6

SEAMLESS HOUSE TRAINING

> *Before you get a dog, you can't quite imagine what living with one might be like; afterward, you can't imagine living any other way.*

— CAROLINE KNAPP

House rules are fundamental in training your puppy. To avoid instances where they show unwanted behavior, they should actually be able to distinguish between what you want them to do, and what not. Because there is no punishment in positive reinforcement training, it can feel hard to set down some solid house rules. In this chapter, we'll be going through everything you need to know about house training within the framework of positive reinforcement.

ESTABLISHING HOUSE RULES

Thinking back to my childhood, I can remember numerous times when my parents enforced a rule that I couldn't understand. In my mind, they were being mean. Now that I'm older, I understand that these rules were for my own safety, development, and good.

Rules are paramount in any household. Whether you and your dog live alone, or you have a house full of people, things would be a complete disaster without rules. Dogs don't adhere to human standards of behavior naturally, so it's important that we teach them what we want them to do.

If you don't have household rules, your pup will revert to its natural instincts, which is not a good thing. Problems like chewing, drinking from the toilet, destroying furniture, and counter surfing are all examples of things that come naturally to dogs that we want to prevent.

Just like with humans, rules are important for your dog's development and safety. Some rules, like *no dogs in the kitchen,* can keep your dog out of harm's way. Other rules, like *no dogs on the furniture,* are there for your own sake.

The rules that you set in your house are completely up to you. Think about what is acceptable behavior in the house and what isn't. You should be very clear about your rules because they will have to be enforced consistently for your dog to catch on and learn them.

If you have other family members in your home, they should be included in the rule-making process. This ensures that everyone is on the same page, and everyone in the home is accommodated. Making clear rules that suit everyone will build a stronger relationship in the family, and avoid conflicts.

Your rules should be written down and placed somewhere where everyone can see them. Make sure that everyone understands all the rules, and keep them simple. You don't want to overcomplicate things, because it can lead to confusion and make it harder for everyone to stick to them.

Everyone in your home should understand the importance of enforcing the rules, not only you. As we've discussed earlier in this book, if everyone isn't consistent with the training, you'll end up confusing your dog more than anything else, leading to bad behavior.

Rules aren't only for your dog. There should be house rules for children, visitors, and anyone in the house to follow. Here are some examples of rules for people:

- **Don't distract the dog while eating.** Some dogs develop aggression when they're bothered during a meal and may want to try and protect their food in unacceptable ways.
- **Be gentle with the puppy.** Children can get quite excited when something as cute as a puppy is in

front of them, which is understandable. However, it's important that they understand that they can seriously hurt the puppy or dog if they are too rough with them. If children are allowed to hurt the dog, it might develop aggression toward children in general.

- **Don't pick up the dog.** I personally enforce this rule with my family, especially with puppies. If we pick them up the wrong way, they can get injured. Unless you have a small dog and everyone knows how to properly pick them up, this is a good rule to enforce.

- **Don't tease the dog.** For children, this is especially important. They don't have to actually hurt the dog to do damage. If they constantly aggravate the dog, you might have a problem with aggression on your hands in the future.

- **No feeding off the table.** We've looked at this rule earlier, but it's so important that everyone agrees on this rule that it's worth mentioning again. Guests should also be aware of this rule.

- **Don't scream at the dog, use negative reinforcement, or physical punishment.** Even though you love your pet, and you plan on changing the way you think to avoid these actions with your dog, it's not enough if only you do it. Everyone in the household should be aware of this rule and stick to it.

- **Who will be assigned to which tasks:** This is an important rule to decide on. Every family is unique, and sometimes, you will have to take full responsibility for your dog. However, in cases where you're the parent and you have children in the house, try to get them as involved as possible by giving them responsibilities toward the dog. Everyone should know exactly what is expected of them.

Now that we've looked at rules for us, we can have a look at rules that you want your dog to follow. Remember that we always want to refrain from shouting *no,* or directing our anger towards our dogs. This can be hard to do when we catch them in the act. With positive reinforcement, we want to give them an alternative activity that suits their need and reward them for stopping the bad behavior.

The first thing to consider when deciding on house rules is safety. Think about all of the places in your home where your pet might get hurt and establish some rules around it. For instance, many dog owners don't allow their dogs in the kitchen because of the hazard of food dropping on the floor, getting stepped on, burnt, or even swallowing something that they shouldn't, like pills.

If you have a swimming pool, you should never let your dog out unsupervised. There are so many cases where dogs are left unattended around swimming pools and end up drowning because they can't get out. You can teach your dog that they're only allowed to be near the pool when you give them a command.

A garage can also be a dangerous place for your dog to be if it's filled with tools or something that can injure them. I think of dogs like children. Their curious nature is a good thing but can get them into trouble sometimes. It's a good idea to keep them out of these areas.

You will have to take the time to evaluate your space thoroughly and identify areas with potential danger. Decide whether you want to keep your dog out of this area completely or let them enter while supervised.

There may be areas in your home that you don't want your dog to enter for other reasons, for example, if you have a family member that has allergies, they may not want the dog to enter their room. You may have a baby room that you don't want them to go into. Whatever the case may be, write down these areas and make sure that everyone in the home agrees about it.

Some people don't allow their dogs on furniture, but it's completely up to you. If your dog is a heavy shedder, you can consider training them to only get on one specific piece of furniture. Whatever you decide to do about the furniture, write it down.

All dogs need basic in-house manners, which may include staying calm and not running up and down with the risk of breaking something, or not jumping on guests or family members. You can teach your dog a cue world like *calm,* or *lay down* to encourage them to calm down.

Don't allow your dog to force their will onto you. Just like you shouldn't force your dog to do things that they don't want to do, they should have the same rule. Your dog may try tugging at your clothes or barking at you to play with them when it's not an appropriate time, and we can train them not to do this by ignoring their behavior and rewarding them once they calm down.

Some dogs get overly excited and jumpy when their food bowl is coming, which is perfectly normal behavior. However, teaching them to calm down and wait until they hear a command to eat is a great way to teach them to act politely and avoid things like jumping on you when food is in its way.

Chewing on anything besides toys is something that you should teach your dog is unacceptable. You don't want to find a surprise like a chewed sofa or table leg, or even shoes for that matter. Implement this rule from a young age for the best results. We'll be looking into this behavior in more detail in the next section.

A good rule to enforce is no running through doors. It may sound strange, but if your dog is left to enter and exit as they please, they may run into glass doors, or even run outside when cars are coming up the driveway. Teach your pup to wait for a command before going through the door for their own safety.

When deciding on rules to make, don't think about your dog as a puppy, but imagine them as an adult. Where a puppy can easily jump up onto your lap and enjoy some lovely belly rubs, it may not be so great when they're a full-grown adult, especially with large and giant breeds. Don't allow your puppy to do things when they're small that will become a nuisance when they're older.

PREVENTING DESTRUCTIVE BEHAVIORS

Dogs were never meant to live indoors with us, and they have natural instincts that don't quite align with our lifestyles. However, being as intelligent as they are, dogs are more than capable of being trained to behave well. We should always try to accommodate their instincts, but at the same time teach them what is acceptable and what is not. In this section, we'll be looking at specific problem behaviors and how we can train our dogs to direct their instincts to more acceptable outlets.

Chewing

Chewing is a perfectly normal behavior for dogs. I can guarantee that your pup will chew on something sometime or another. However, there are a few cases when a dog may become what I call a *serial chewer*, and nothing is safe from those sharp teeth.

Both in the puppy and adult stages of life, it's necessary for your dog to chew. Chewing makes their jaws stronger and also helps relieve some pain when they have new teeth coming out (*Destructive Chewing*, n.d.). Chewing is not the problem, but chewing the wrong things is.

Your dog may chew on objects other than their toys for several reasons, including boredom, frustration, anxiety, a lack of the right toys, or even just for fun. The first step in getting your dog to stop chewing on things they shouldn't is to ensure that they have a variety of chew toys that they enjoy chewing.

The toys that you provide for your dog must be safe and suitable for them. Never give your dog something that they can potentially swallow or bite pieces off to swallow. Not only is this a choking hazard, but if the toy becomes lodged in their intestines, they may need an operation to remove it, or it can be life-threatening. An operation to remove something from the intestines is a risky one, so it's better to avoid it altogether.

Many give their dogs bones to chew on, which is a big no-no. Bones can have sharp edges and can damage the intestines if swallowed. Not only can bones also get lodged in the intestines, but there is a risk of necrosis of the intestinal walls if it's damaged by sharp edges.

Go for hard rubber, strong chew toys that can't be chewed in half. Always supervise your dog when chewing on their toys, and rather throw away a toy that's coming apart to stop them from ingesting pieces of it. Rawhide is safe in most cases but shouldn't be given to your dog unsupervised. Also, make sure that you get the rawhide from a vet shop, and ask your veterinarian if it is safe for your dog. Always ensure that soft toys have non-toxic fillings and fix or discard them when they start coming apart.

If your dog is a serial chewer, try to confine them to an area in the house where you can keep an eye on them while training them to stop chewing. Never leave clothes, shoes, or other items that may be attractive for them to chew out in the open. Make sure that you *dog-proof* your home and put away anything that can be chewed on. Make sure that the trash bin and laundry basket are out of reach for your pup, as these are some problem areas that many dog owners experience.

Because dogs may chew something out of boredom, ensure that you give them enough mental stimulation during the day. If you're busy, give them something like a food puzzle to play with to keep them occupied. While a puppy is teething, they will inevitably look for something to chew to ease their discomfort. You can provide them with a chew toy that can be frozen, or even a little bit of frozen fruit. Puppies will stop teething at around six months old, so ensure that you train them on chewing during this time to avoid habitual chewing.

If you find your dog chewing something they're not supposed to, the key is to stay calm. It can be very frustrating, but trying to fish something out of their mouths or chasing them may feel like a game to them. Don't approach your dog, but let them come to you. If you approach them first, they can start showing signs of guarding behavior, because they'll know that you want to take something from them. The right way to do it is to find them the appropriate object to chew and trade with them. Reward them when they take the toy from you.

Your dog may be reluctant to give up whatever they're chewing, so you might need to try and lure them away with a treat or two. Make sure that you discard the bits of whatever they were chewing. If their chewing on things like furniture persists, you can try getting some chew-deterrent spray. These sprays are invented to keep your dog from chewing on things without harming them. The worst that they get out of it is a bad smell and a funky taste in their mouths.

Never offer your dog something that you don't want them to chew in the future, like old socks or clothes. They might think that it's okay to chew these items in the future. Always stick to high-quality, safe options, and keep in mind that it will take time for them to know what they're allowed to chew and what not. Rotate their chew toys now and then to keep things fresh, and stay consistent with your training.

Chewing can also be the result of separation anxiety. I've seen many cases where dog owners are afraid to leave their pets at home for fear of them destroying something. Separation anxiety is something that can be treated, but we have to be patient. Try playing with your dog before leaving, and remember to remove all chewable objects. If you tire them out before leaving, it can help them get rid of some of the frustration.

Overall, chewing shouldn't be viewed as a bad thing. Your dog is only doing what their instincts are telling them to. Chewing is a good thing and can help keep their teeth and gums healthy. Don't punish them for doing what they're naturally inclined to do, but rather teach them how to do it acceptably.

Digging

There are few things as fun as rolling around in some fresh dirt and digging up a storm for most dogs. However, it's not fun for us when they happen to dig up our freshly planted petunias in the process. Digging can cause a lot of frustration, not only for gardeners but for any dog owner. Holes all over the backyard pose a safety risk. Trust me, I've tripped in enough of them to know.

Dogs dig for different reasons, and knowing your dog well will help you better understand why they do it, and help you prevent this behavior. Some dogs dig holes out of boredom and a lack of enrichment. You can prevent this by providing them with plenty of enriching toys and spending time with them.

Your dog may need to get rid of some extra energy, and some breeds are more prone to digging than others. They can also learn this behavior from other dogs. Make sure that your dog gets enough exercise and is always mentally stimulated.

If you're an avid gardener, your dog may try to imitate your behavior. If they see you working in the soil, they will try do to the same. It's important to understand that your dog is not digging with any ill intentions, and we can't punish them for it. Consider getting something like a sand pit where they're allowed to dig and reward them when they dig in this area instead of in the garden.

Your dog may be searching for prey if your yard has moles or rodents. In this case, you will have to get rid of the infestation, or your dog might not stop this behavior. Never place any poison or other harmful substances in the yard, as this will not only harm the moles or rodents but also your dog.

If you find your dog digging, you can distract them with something else like a toy or teach them to respond to a recall command. Once they stop this behavior and turn their attention toward you, you can reward them.

Your dog may dig holes to lay down in for comfort, which may mean that you're not providing them with an alternative comfortable spot to lie in. Make sure that they have a safe space that is protected from the elements where they can go to escape excessive heat or cold.

Anxiety can play a role in digging, and spending enough time with your pup can help avoid this behavior. Pregnant dogs may show nesting behavior and dig holes when they're near the end of their gestation period. Provide them with an alternative comfortable place to lay in.

Some dogs are what I like to refer to as *escape artists*, and they dig holes near the fence to try and escape the yard. This can happen because they want to try and find you when you're not home, they are traumatized and anxious, or they may even just be curious. If your dog digs when you're not home, it might be a good idea to place them in a crate for short periods while you running errands.

Dogs that have a history of trauma may try to escape when newly adopted. If this is the case, you might need to limit their outside access when unsupervised until they feel more comfortable in your home. If you have a high-energy, curious dog that likes digging near fences, you can try tiring them out a bit more to get rid of their excess energy with playtime or a walk. Place some heavy rocks near your fence or bury your fence a few feet into the soil to prevent your dog from digging a hole under it and escaping. The environment that you keep your dog in should always be comfortable and inviting to them.

While we should always understand that this behavior is natural for our dogs, we should do everything from our side that we can to keep them out of trouble. You may want to consider fencing off your garden beds if the digging in them persists.

Scratching the Floor

Some dogs tend to scratch floors in conjunction with digging, which we want to avoid to keep our floors in good condition. As with digging, scratching can be a way of keeping themselves occupied when bored, anxious, or even in pain.

Always keep your dog exercised and stimulated with fun activities, and give them a comfortable, safe place to lie in. Apart from that, you can use the same method as with digging for training. Distract them from scratching and reward them once they stop.

To avoid your floors getting damaged, cut their nails regularly. Any sand, hair, or other debris on the flooring can scratch or damage it when stepped on, so try to sweep the floor regularly. You can also routinely wax your floor. If unwanted behavior continues despite all of your efforts, you can consider consulting a veterinarian or animal behavioral specialist.

At the end of the day, we have to share our home with our best friends, and it's our responsibility to teach them the right behavior. Doing this will help us create a peaceful, harmonious environment for us, our family, and our dogs. In the next chapter, we'll be learning about the importance of socialization and adaptation in positive reinforcement training, and how to implement it into your daily training routine.

7

SOCIALIZATION AND ADAPTATION

> *Fall in love with a dog, and in many ways, you enter a new orbit, a universe that features not just new colors but new rituals, new rules, a new way of experiencing attachment.*
>
> — CAROLINE KNAPP

Socialization refers to introducing your dog to different people, situations, and animals in a safe, controlled way. A dog that is fearful and anxious is often unpredictable, and we can't blame them for it, because humans are the same. We've all had anxiety about a new situation at some time or another, so we know what it feels like. Now, imagine having that anxiety and fear, and you can't understand what's going on. All you have to rely on is someone else. This is how our dogs feel.

We have the responsibility to protect our dogs in all situations, and by socializing them we can do this with more confidence. For example, a dog that is fearful of traffic might pull the leash out of your hands and run off when a car approaches. This is an extremely dangerous scenario, and proper socialization could help you avoid such instances.

In this Chapter, we'll be looking into what socialization looks like for your dog, and how their unique personalities will play an important role in how you approach it. With the right socialization training, the world is your oyster. Let's get right into it!

THE IMPORTANCE OF SOCIALIZATION

All dogs are unique, as we've learned thus far. This means that they will have unique fears and sources of anxiety. There is no *one-size-fits-all* regarding what they can be afraid of, which is why we should expose our pets to as many different scenarios as possible at a young age.

If we want our dogs to do well in our homes and society, socializing is crucial. Aggression and skittish behavior often stem from fear of the unknown in dogs. If our dogs are exposed to different people and animals at a young age, they're less likely to behave undesirably around them. Everyone loves a friendly dog, and life can be so much more enjoyable.

If your dog is properly socialized, you can take them on trips with you, walk them confidently, and just let them experience more overall. Besides this, your dog won't be enjoying themselves if they feel fearful all the time. We want them to live a full, happy life, and good socialization just makes that a bigger possibility. Their mental and physical health will benefit greatly from not feeling unsure and scared all the time.

Dangerous situations can stem from dogs that are not socialized with other dogs. There have been countless cases of dogs attacking other dogs, and injuring other people, themselves, and even their owners due to a lack of socialization. It's never a pretty picture, and things can get serious quickly. Thus, for their safety and the safety of other pet owners and their pets, we have a responsibility to make sure that our dogs know how to behave around others.

If you have other dogs in the house or plan on getting another dog down the line, socialization will teach your pup how to act appropriately around them. Fighting over resources and guarding behavior are some of the things that happen when they're not taught these valuable social skills and can lead to conflict in your home.

Not only will your dog need at least two routine checkups from the vet yearly, but sometimes the unforeseen happens and you can find yourself with an injured dog. Vet visits are almost always stressful for our pets, which is why socializing them is important to help alleviate some of it. If your dog is uncontrollable around other people, including the vet, it will make it that much harder for them to get the medical attention that they need.

The same goes for grooming. You don't want your dog to injure the groomer or other dogs, or be overly anxious and fearful. As we've seen in Chapter 1, grooming is paramount to your dog's routine care. If your dog is unable to be groomed professionally, it can make things a lot harder for you.

Overall, a socialized dog is a happy dog. We've all most likely encountered a pet owner with a dog that isn't properly socialized and seen the consequences. From excessive barking to aggression to urination out of fear when they encounter new people, all of this is avoidable. An unsocialized dog causes unnecessary stress for the family and others. By teaching your dog the right behavior in new situations, you can help them build confidence and strengthen your bond.

Everyone's experience with their dog will be unique, and you might have adopted an adult dog instead of starting with a puppy. When adopting a dog, we often don't know their history or what they've been exposed to. They might have had bad experiences with other humans or dogs which has led them to be traumatized, anxious, or even aggressive.

I don't believe in the saying—*old dogs can't learn new tricks.* Dogs of all ages can be rehabilitated and socialized with the right amount of consistency, patience, and love. Socializing a puppy takes a lot of patience, but even more so with an adult. Socializing should ideally be done before the age of four months, which makes it even more challenging to socialize an adult.

It can take weeks, months, or even years in some cases to break through to some adult dogs that have been traumatized in the past. However, don't let this get you down. I promise you that your patience and kindness toward your dog will be rewarded tenfold when they start trusting you and being confident in unknown situations. Without you, that dog might have gone their entire life being fearful and anxious, all alone. Just keep going, even if you feel like nothing is working. We'll be going deeper into socializing your dog in specific situations in the next section.

When I was younger, I had a close friend who volunteered at a local no-kill shelter that doubled as a veterinary office. They were short-staffed most of the time, so she felt a need to help them out as much as she could. They often gave free medical treatment to pets whose owners couldn't afford medical care, which made it even more worthwhile for her.

There were a few cases of aggression that she came across in her time there, but none as bad as their most infamous client, Simba. Simba was a massive male Rottweiler, and the moment his owners came through the doors, you could see the staff's faces drop. Some of them even miraculously found something more important to do at that exact moment that they needed assistance.

Simba was completely unsocialized with other animals and people, and he was an absolute nightmare for the vet to work with. They would bring him in a large steel wire cage on the back of their pickup truck, and the vet would have to find creative ways to inject him with a local anesthetic without losing a hand or a few fingers each time.

Animals can't talk to us and tell us how they're feeling, or where it hurts. A vet has one of the hardest jobs out there because they have to figure out what's based on nothing but the owner's observations and the dog's reaction to certain touches and actions. They have to figure out which tests to do and how to treat something with this information. Vets often need to rely on a dog's reaction or flinch when being examined to have an idea of where the pain is. If a dog is under anesthetic while being examined, it can make an accurate diagnosis much harder.

There was an incident where one of the volunteers got bitten on the hand by Simba and had to get stitches. She quit on the spot, making the shelter even more short-staffed than it already was. The point is, it wasn't Simba's fault. He was fearful of seeing other people and being transported in a cage on the back of a pickup truck because he was completely isolated on a farm his entire life. All Simba was, was afraid. It has nothing to do with his size or breed, but it was because of the lack of socialization.

INTRODUCING NEW SITUATIONS

New Dogs

While a puppy, introduce your dog to as many new friends as possible. Puppy classes from a trainer who uses positive reinforcement training are a great way to do this. Your puppy will have the opportunity to interact with different dogs from different breeds and backgrounds in a controlled, supervised environment.

Taking them on a trip to the dog park often also helps with socialization. Unlike with puppy classes, your dog will meet dogs of all different ages and stages in socialization. This might seem frightening for them at first, but keep rewarding them for positive interactions, and they will eventually warm up.

As your puppy gets older, they will start to discover more of their personalities and fears. If you socialize them well from the beginning, they're less likely to fear other dogs or become aggressive when they're around. However, it's not impossible for them to develop a sudden dislike or fear of other dogs around the age of five months or so.

If this happens, just continue exposing them to other dogs in a controlled, safe way. Reward them for good behavior, and when they're paying more attention to you than other dogs. Soon enough they will associate meeting other dogs and being polite with good experiences and rewards.

Adult dogs find it a bit more challenging to socialize with other pets if they haven't had too many experiences, or positive experiences overall, with other dogs. Remember to make small advances in socializing, allowing them to move at their own pace. If your dog seems too anxious or frustrated at the dog park, rather take them home than overwhelm them. Consider setting up meetings with a friend who has a well-socialized and trained dog.

If your dog is showing aggressive body language, direct their attention toward something else. Aggressive body language includes stiff posture, low-hanging head, snarling, low-hanging tail, or raised hair on the back of their necks. Remember not to punish your dog for this or yell at them, but simply redirect their attention.

The moment the aggressive stance eases up, you can reward them. When introducing another dog to yours, do it in a neutral place where neither one of them can claim it as their territory. This can include any quiet, safe outdoor spot. Keep both dogs on a leash to have a bit more control over the situation.

The other handler should be knowledgeable about the dog's body language and be able to spot when the dog is behaving aggressively. Walk in the same direction with both dogs, but far apart enough for them not to take too much notice of each other. Keep rewarding your dog when he walks calmly and ignores the other dog.

You can start moving a little bit closer to each other as your dog eases up more. When they resume an aggressive stance, move further apart again. Repeat this and reward your dog when he stays calm. This may take a few tries, and you won't necessarily be able to introduce them to the new dog at close range in the first walk.

Don't make these sessions too long, as that may cause your dog to become frustrated. Keep sessions short and productive. Eventually, you will be able to move closer to the other owner and their dog and walk them side by side. Once they're comfortable doing this, they can be allowed to sniff and become familiar with each other.

Don't place your expectations for an adult dog too high. Even if they can only become socialized with one other dog at first, it's a step in the right direction. Let them take their time to overcome their fear and anxiety, and don't push them too hard. Your next step will be organizing supervised play dates for the pups. Remove anything that they can fight over out of the environment, and let them get to know each other.

As you take your dog for walks, they will most likely come into contact with other dogs. This is also a great way to train socialization. You can use the same rewarding method, and reward them when they show positive, relaxed behavior.

Introducing a new dog into your home can be challenging if you already own an adult dog that has been a *single child* for a while. It's important to take into account that dogs can become jealous of each other for your attention, and also show guarding and territorial behavior. This is why the first impressions matter.

Use the same method of introducing them on neutral grounds outdoors. Don't take them both into your home immediately. Once they've met outside, you can take them to your yard, or a large space, where you and someone assisting you can supervise their interaction.

Keep an eye out for any unwanted behavior and redirect their attention or stop the interaction once things look like they're about to go South. When they're comfortable with each other outside, it's time to take them into your home. Remove food bowls, toys, and anything else that might cause conflict.

Each dog should have their own safe space and crate or bed. In the first few weeks, keep them separated unless supervised. Also, keep their interactions with each other short and fun, and reward them for good behavior. They will need some time apart in the beginning to avoid frustration with each other.

Always feed them in separate areas, and don't forget to spend some alone time with each dog from time to time. If a scuffle occurs, separate them for a day or two. This will help them manage the stress, and they can be reintroduced once they've had their off time. When leaving home, always separate them until you're completely confident that they are used to each other.

Although it may be a long, tiresome process sometimes, socializing your pet is for the best. Their well-being and quality of life depend on it, and with enough love, grace, and patience, you will be well on your way to a harmonious lifestyle with your dog.

Other People

Your dog will meet new people almost every day when you take them for a walk. Ensuring that they know how to behave will allow you to experience so much more with them. If dogs aren't socialized to other people, they can either become overexcited and jump on them causing a nuisance, or they can be fearful and aggressive.

An unsocialized dog can be a problem if you receive guests or visit others. You want your guests to feel comfortable coming into your home, without a dog barking at them or scaring them. In the same way, we also want our dogs to feel comfortable around others and not anxious. As we've discussed, this can help your dog get medical attention from a vet or be groomed without hassle.

It's ideal to socialize your dog with other people as a puppy to help them understand that other humans don't pose a threat. Let others play with your puppy, and give them the commands that you use. Let the stranger give them plenty of treats and affection, and reward your dog if they're following the commands and showing good behavior.

If your puppy is shy, always let them decide whether they want to interact or not. It's important not to overwhelm them. Let the dog initiate the interaction, and let the person give them treats. This will help your pup associate reward with positive interactions with other humans.

Things get a little bit more complicated when we're dealing with an adult dog. They might have had a bad experience in the past, which led them to believe that all other humans are bad. This shows in the way they interact with people. They can either bark and become aggressive, cower and hide behind you, or even urinate out of fear.

Before introducing someone to your dog at home, you should give them a head's up on what they should and shouldn't do, especially with a fearful, anxious dog:

- Do not make direct eye contact. This is seen as a threat.
- Let your guest acknowledge you, ignoring the dog at first.
- Do not reach out to the dog or try to initiate an interaction.
- Do not speak loudly or make sudden, frightening moves.
- Stay calm.
- You can tell your guest some of your command words like *sit* before they meet your dog.
- Let the dog sniff you, and keep still.

When the guest arrives, your dog must be in the heel position, or given a command to sit or lay down. Always keep your dog on a leash during first introductions. Greet your guest with a handshake, and reward your dog if they're calm. Once you've all settled down and taken a seat, you can give your guest some treats to offer your dog.

Let the guest toss some treats toward the dog gently, without making eye contact. Each toss can be closer to the guest. If your dog is not a biter, you can eventually let your guests offer them a treat by hand. Always watch your dog's body language for aggression, fear, or anxiety.

Your dog may begin to warm up to your guest, taking treats from their hand. Once they're comfortable enough with your guest to do this, let your guest stop giving them treats. This will give your dog the chance to walk over to the guest voluntarily and seek attention because they think they will get a treat. If this is the case, your guest may slowly pet your dog's side or back, but never the head.

If your dog continues protective, aggressive, or fearful behavior despite your efforts, stop the interaction. Give them a break from the guest, and let them go to their safe spot. It will take time and patience for your dog to become used to strangers, but you have to keep trying. Eventually, they will warm up. Just stay consistent.

When it comes to meeting strangers in the street or at the dog park, you must know which stage your dog is with their socialization, and what they can handle. In the beginning stages, your dog may feel comfortable enough to stand close to a stranger but might bite if someone tries to touch them. The better you know your dog and observe their behavior, the better your understanding will be of what makes them uncomfortable.

If a stranger approaches you and your dog, politely give them boundaries before they have the chance to interact with your dog. Most people will ask you if they can pet your dog, but some people might try to pet them without permission. If your dog is anxious around other people, this can be a stressful situation for them. Politely say something like "She's shy, please don't pet her", or "He's not friendly, sorry."

What you say will depend on your dog's boundaries. If your dog is in the appropriate stage of their socialization, you can ask the stranger to let them sniff their shoes, or even let them offer your dog a treat. The key is to closely supervise your dog and read their body language at all times throughout any interaction.

New Environment

Introducing your dog to a new environment can be very stressful, or even exciting for them. They will be bombarded with all kinds of smells and sounds, and because their senses are so sharp, it can quickly become scary and overwhelming for them.

The most important thing to remember is that they need time. Time to listen, smell, and see the new space. This may be a dog park, a new home, or even a holiday destination. Before taking your dog to the dog park, they should be trained to do a recall and have a level of socialization with other dogs.

Keep your dog on a leash for the first few visits to the park until they feel comfortable. They will most likely have some sort of reaction the first time, as there are many smells and sounds of other dogs. This can include excitedly jumping, barking, or acting fearful. It's perfectly normal for them.

Before entering the park, allow your dog to calm down. Reward them when they're calm. When entering, keep an eye on their body language. Once they've taken in all of the smells and sounds, you can start moving into the park slowly. Keep rewarding your dog for good behavior throughout the whole process.

When visiting new locations for the first time, always try to go during the quietest times of the day and week. This will help your dog get used to the space without too many distractions. In the beginning, take them for short periods until they feel comfortable to spend more time in the area.

Busy streets can be very stressful for your dog, and depending on where you live, you will have to introduce them to these areas. If your dog shows signs of fear, barks, or does anything unwanted, distract them with a command like *sit* and reward them when they comply. They will begin to associate the area with reward and warm up to it. You may have to do this numerous times before your dog is comfortable.

Try to expose your dog to as many new areas as possible often to help them build more confidence. They will eventually gain enough confidence and trust in you that they won't be too afraid of new areas, and they'll know how to behave. The time you spend socializing your dog in new areas is precious and can help build a stronger relationship.

MANAGING FEAR AND ANXIETY

To understand how to manage fear and anxiety in dogs, we need to take a thorough look at the signs thereof to be able to identify them. While there are many signs to look for, it's important to note that these signs can present themselves differently in each dog. You may see multiple signs being portrayed at once, or one subtle sign. This is why we should always observe our dog's reactions to everything, subtle as they might be. This can help us understand what their specific signs of fear and anxiety are.

Some behaviors such as trembling, cowering, hiding behind an owner, and urination can be obvious indicators of fear and anxiety. Other behaviors like lip-licking, yawning, and avoiding eye contact are less obvious but should be noted. A fearful dog may drop their ears and hang their heads low, tuck their tails between their legs, and try to run away.

If your dog is extremely fearful, they might bark, bite, howl, pant, and pace up and down. Destructive behavior is also an indicator of fear and anxiety. Some dogs will go as far as injuring themselves by biting or scratching. A dog that hides or continuously tries to escape a situation can be deemed anxious.

At the shelter where my friend volunteered, the vet taught them to look out for a *whale eye* in dogs. A whale eye refers to dilated pupils, and being able to see the whites of a dog's eyes excessively. They may give you a side stare, showing the whites of their eyes. This is an indication of fear, and it's best to steer clear of a dog giving you the whale eye, as it may try to bite you. Growling and aggressive behavior can also stem from fear and anxiety.

Some dogs may develop phobias for things like thunder, lawnmowers, or even vacuum cleaners. Other dogs have a fear of confinement, and won't tolerate being crated. All dogs are different, but the way we treat fear of certain things stays the same. If your dog is showing fearful behavior, distract them with a command and a treat. Depending on how bad the fear is, this may take many tries before they calm down.

With any fear-related behavior, consistency is key. Your dog may look to you for protection in times when they feel unsafe or vulnerable, and you will have to comfort them while continuing with training. Always keep your voice soft and friendly, and give them a lot of praise and reward when they redirect their attention to you instead of the source of fear.

Anxiety is more profound in some dog breeds such as Toy Poodles and Cocker Spaniels. Before getting a dog, make sure that you do enough research on common problems that the breed may have. In some breeds, the wrong situations can aggravate their anxiety to a level where medical intervention is necessary.

Dogs that don't seem to get better, even with a lot of consistent training, will need to see a professional. This is usually a last resort, and your veterinary behaviorist or vet can help you with a few more techniques to try depending on your dog's unique personality and situation.

In extreme cases of anxiety, the vet may prescribe some anti-anxiety medication for your dog. This can be a permanent or temporary thing depending on your dog's profile. There are natural anti-anxiety products that are available over the counter at most vet shops, but it doesn't work in all situations. Always make sure that you know exactly what is in the product, its effects, the dosage, and how long you can use it. Always consult a professional about natural products before giving them to your dog.

At the end of the day, not socializing your dog to new people, environments, and animals, will certainly lead to fear and anxiety. The more you can expose them to at a young age, the more confident they will be. Even if older dogs may take longer to become comfortable, consistently sticking to training will make a big difference.

HOW TO DEAL WITH BARKING

Dogs communicate different messages with us through barking. Although it may become an inconvenience for us when they start barking excessively, we should under-stand that it's completely normal behavior and we can't expect them to stop barking altogether.

There is a difference between occasional barking when they're trying to tell us something, and excessive barking when they're alone or bored. Dogs will bark at things that frighten them, which can be distinguished by their body language while doing so. Dogs that bark out of fear will show anxious behavior, with rigid bodies and hanging ears.

This is an important indication for us, and we should never punish or yell at them for barking out of fear. If we know what frightens them, we can better manage their fear in the future by either removing the source of fear or implementing socialization training to help them overcome it.

Some dogs bark when left alone due to separation anxiety. When left alone or confined, they can quickly pick up bad habits. This can cause disturbances for your neighbors, which we want to avoid. If you know that your dog barks constantly when you're not around, tire them out before leaving. A lot of energy can lead to a lot of barking, so giving them some exercise or play time before you leave can help you overcome this.

It's also possible that dogs start barking excessively due to chronic pain or discomfort. Dogs are territorial animals and will bark aggressively when a stranger is entering their territory.

Barking excessively becomes a habit if you don't nip it in the bud. It's best to start training them in this regard as soon as possible. As with all training, consistency is needed to imbed the right behavior.

Identifying the reason why your dog is barking can help you prevent it. For instance, if your dog is barking at something outside the window, close the curtains and reward them once they calm down. Always do everything from your side to minimize the barking, even if it's something like removing an item that is aggravating them. Teaching them a command like *stop* or *quiet* when you want your dog to stop barking can help them better understand what you expect of them.

To do this, intervene when your dog is barking. Say the command word, and once your dog turns their attention to you, reward them. If they stop barking for a bit at any stage after hearing the command word, reward them immediately before they start again. They will begin to associate the command with reward and catch on sooner or later. You will have to do this several times and stay consistent.

Sometimes it's like second nature to shout the command when you feel frustrated with the barking, but this is definitely not a good idea. Punishment will have the opposite of the desired effect in this regard. Your dog may think that you're also *barking*, and never get the message. It's important that you say the command word in a calm tone of voice. Diverting their attention is a great way to teach them to ignore whatever it is that they're barking at.

If the barking persists, consult a veterinarian. Your dog may be experiencing some sort of discomfort, like arthritis, or even a form of senility in older dogs. Your vet will be able to rule anything clinical out for you if you're worried. They will also be able to give you some advice more specific to your situation.

Every dog will have different habits and problems, but the important thing is that we keep on with training no matter what. With socialization and problem behavior, we have to make sure that everyone who spends time with your dog is aware of their stage in training, and also follows it. In the next chapter, we'll be going over some basic commands that you can teach your dog.

8

BASIC DOG COMMANDS

> *If you have a dog, you will most likely outlive it; to get a dog is to open yourself to profound joy and, prospectively, to equally profound sadness.*
>
> — MARJORIE GARBER

We use commands in positive reinforcement training to queue certain actions that we want our dogs to do. By giving them a sound to recognize and associate with action and reward, we can help them understand exactly what we expect of them. Commands also make it much easier to control a situation and work on further training.

In some situations, we rely on commands to keep our dogs safe. In the case of a recall command, we use it to call our dogs back when they wander off too far or if we notice potential danger. We also use commands to distract our dogs from things that might frighten them or make them anxious.

A dog that knows his commands is well-disciplined. Teaching your dog commands can help you shape good behavior in your dog in a fun, interactive way. While each dog owner can create the commands that work for them, we'll be looking at a few options in this book, and how to teach them to your dog. After this chapter, you will be able to train your dog to follow some of the most important commands with confidence, as well as a few extras.

NO

This command is one of the most used commands in the household. There will always be certain unacceptable behaviors, and your dog needs to understand when you want them to stop with something.

The misconception is that you have to yell at your dog to get them to stop what they're doing when this is not the right way to do it. We might slip up a few times, and that's okay. You will learn with your pup. When using the *No, or Leave it,* command, always do so in a calm, but assertive way. The moment you frighten your dog by shouting, the training is ineffective.

This command, unlike some other commands, will be used in many different scenarios. Whether they're jumping on someone, tugging at something, or trying to jump on the counter, this command comes in handy. Because it's carried out in so many different situations, it can take a while before your dog understands what you mean by it. This is also why choosing one word is best to avoid confusion.

To start training this command, show them a treat with your left hand. Once they come closer to take the treat from you, close your hand and say the command. You can allow them to come near your hand and sniff it, but don't let them take the treat. It may feel like some dogs are relentless for their treats, and won't stop trying to get it. However, they will get bored at some stage or another, and focus their attention on something else.

Once they do this, reward them with a treat. Be sure to use your right hand this time. This may seem confusing to them at first, but stay patient. This is the easiest way to teach them what the command means. Once they understand that they're not supposed to try getting the treat from your hand when you've spoken the command, they will likely wait for you to give it to them instead of licking or sniffing your hand. When you've reached this point in training, you can start using the command in other scenarios.

When your dog does something that you don't want them to do, calmly say the command. Make sure that they can hear you. The moment they stop and turn their attention toward you, reward them. This can be done with any action that you don't want them to do, which means that you can potentially work on this training every day. With consistency in rewards, they will quickly learn what the command means.

WAIT OR STAY

These commands are two very helpful commands with two different meanings. Stay is used when you want your dog to calmly stay in a position until you return to them. Wait is used to let them know that they have to stay in position temporarily and wait for you to give them another command.

While these commands have different meanings, they're trained in a very similar way. *Stay* is trained first, and w*ait* is trained thereafter. If your dog has the foundation of the *stay* command, it will make it much easier for them to understand the *wait* command.

The *wait* command is used when you want your dog to be calm while they're expecting further instruction. Before you put their food down, teaching them to *wait* before they dive right in can help them calm down enough and learn not to jump on you or tug at your clothes while you on your way to their bowl.

You can also use the *wait* command before going through a door. Tell them to wait, and use a release word to let them know that they can go through the door. Your release word should always stay the same. Something like *go* or *okay* can be used when you want to release your dog from their position.

The stay command can be used when you want to cross the road for a quick errand or go into an area where dogs aren't allowed, such as the baby's room in your home. Your dog will understand that they need to wait for you to come back and give them the release command before they can follow you.

To teach your dog to stay, let them sit. Once they sit, wait a few seconds, and reward them. Start saying *stay* after they sit, and try to let them sit a bit longer each time before you reward them. When they're comfortable with sitting for a while before being rewarded, you can try moving away one step, and if they stay in position, reward them.

Move away a bit further each time. Eventually, they will understand that stay means that you want them to hold their position while you move away. Now you can start teaching them the release word. After they've stayed, walk back to them and say the release word in a high-pitched, excited tone. This will likely make them move to you. You can reward them once they do.

Keep doing these exercises consistently. When they've grasped the concept of stay, you can teach them to wait. Instead of saying stay, say wait. Move away a little bit, and give them the release word. You can move further and further away, giving them the release word when you're at a distance. Reward them if they come to you. If they walk to you without the release word at any stage, take them back to where you began, and start again.

DOWN

This command is used in settings where you need your dog to be calm, out of the way, and lie down. You might be receiving guests, working on something dangerous, climbing on a ladder, or getting the mail from the mailman. Whatever the situation, this command is handy to teach during training.

To teach your dog this command, they will need to be in a sitting position. Bring a treat to their nose to let them smell it, and close your hand. Move your hand to their paws slowly, making sure to move it close to their chest. Hold the treat between their paws so that they follow it with their nose. Move your hand away from them slowly, and once they lay down, give them the treat and praise them.

This may take a few tries before they understand, but stay consistent. Once they can lie down for the treat, start saying the word *down* as they do so to help them associate the word with the action. You can do this training after exercise, or when your dog is tired to make it easier to get them to lie down. When they lie down by themselves during the day, say the command and reward them.

SIT

Sitting is one of the first and easiest commands that you will teach your dog. This command is used as a foundation for many other commands and can help you train them easier in the future. This is also a useful command to use when you want your dog to calm down, or when you want to distract them from something.

While your dog is standing, take a treat and hold it over their nose. Move your hand toward their tail, and once they sit down, give them the treat and praise. Do this a few times, and then start saying the command the moment they sit down. After a few repetitions, try saying the command and then offering the treat.

WATCH ME

There are certain situations when you will need to have your dog's unwavering attention, and the *watch me* command can help you achieve this. While socializing your dog, this is a great command to use to get their attention on you instead of whatever's making them nervous.

This command is beneficial during training and can help them learn faster. If you know that your dog is focusing on you, you can be certain that they will take in much more information.

To teach your dog this command, show them a treat and let them sniff it. bring the treat toward your face to your forehead. It helps if your dog is in the sitting position when you do this. Your dog will most likely focus on the treat. Once they focus solely on the treat, reward and praise them.

Start by doing this while close to your dog, and move a bit further away each time. Make sure that you hold the treat in front of your face for long enough for them to understand that you want them to look at you. As the training progresses, you can start saying the command while doing this. Your dog will eventually associate the command with making eye contact with you, and your training will be successful. Feel free to start making a hand gesture toward your eyes during training to further clarify the communication.

SPEAK

The *speak* command essentially teaches your dog to bark when you give them the cue word. This isn't a practical command, but quite a fun one to work on. Achieving this with your dog will give you a great sense of accomplishment, and it's a great party trick!

This command requires a lot of patience and good timing. Show your dog a treat, but close your fist so they won't be able to take it. Stand still and wait. Your dog will grow impatient eventually and may bark at you to let you know about it. The moment your dog barks, reward them with the treat.

Try this a few times before giving them the command with the action. It's important that you keep an eye on them and say the command right before they're about to bark. When you've done this a few times, you can start by saying the command word, and reward them when they respond with a bark. This command doesn't always work for all dogs, but you have a great chance of teaching it to your pup if you stay consistent.

DROP IT

This command, like many others, is mainly taught for your dog's safety. There will undoubtedly be a time when your dog has something in their mouth that they're not supposed to, which is where the *drop-it* cue comes in. This cue tells your dog that they have to drop whatever they have in their mouth immediately.

The moment you start chasing your dog with whatever they have in their mouth, they think that you're playing a game with them. This might encourage them to continue the behavior and do it more often. The *drop-it* cue will

138 | SANDRA FELLERS

allow you to retrieve whatever they're harboring in their mouth without encouraging bad behavior.

To teach your dog to drop items on command, you will need a toy and they're favorite treats. When they've played with their toy for a while, crouch down to their level and offer them the treat. When they release the toy and take the treat, praise them. You can give them back their toy and repeat the process a few times.

Once your dog understands this concept, start using your command word with the action. If he responds to the command, reward and praise. After a few sessions, you'll be able to say the command without offering them a treat, and they will drop whatever they have in their mouth.

UP OR STAND

This command is used when you want your dog to stand up, and stay in position. It can come in handy in many situations during training, and also in everyday life around the house. This command is essentially the opposite of *sit*, which means that we train it the opposite way.

While your dog is sitting down, bring a treat close to their nose, and move backward. They will most likely try to follow the treat and stand up. Reward them the moment they do so, and repeat a few times, adding the command right before they stand up. Once they're comfortable doing so, you can give them the command without the treat but always praise.

BACK

This command is used when you want your dog to back up a bit from a certain area or object. It can help you keep them safe from hazardous situations like someone passing by quickly with a bike, or even if they're just in the way of something that you're trying to reach. Using the *back* cue instead of pushing them out of the way or any similar action is much more effective.

Take a treat in your hand, and walk toward your dog. Move close enough for them to take a step backward. Once they do this, reward them. Move away from your dog, and repeat. You can start using the *back* cue right before you walk toward them. Keep repeating this exercise until they back up on command without you having to walk toward them.

ROLL OVER

Rolling over is simply a fun trick to teach your dog. Your dog loves playing and training with you, and they will enjoy this just as much as you will. Your heart is guaranteed to melt the first time your pup successfully does a rollover!

Before teaching your dog the *rollover* cue, teach them the *down* cue to make it easier for them. Try starting your rollover training on a soft surface like grass so they don't hurt themselves on the first few attempts.

Give your dog the *down* cue, and reward them when they complete it. You will need some high-value treats. Once your dog is in the down position, take the treat and hold it in front of their nose, moving it toward their shoulder slowly. They should lay on their side when you do this. When they do, reward them. You will have to practice this repetitively before moving on to the next step.

The next step is to hold the treat close to their nose and move it slowly to the back of their head. This will encourage them to roll over their entire body. It might take a few tries for them to understand what you want them to do, but once they do, keep encouraging this movement with reward and praise.

Once they can do this, you can do the entire thing in one movement, having them go from *down* to laying on their side, and then rolling over. The moment they can do this movement all together, introduce your command right before they do so. This is a difficult command for your dog to learn, so remember to be patient as it may take quite a few tries.

JUMP

Teaching your dog to jump on command has more value than merely being a good party trick. I believe that this command is essential, especially for large breed dogs. There will be times when you will need to get them on a platform like the back of a pickup truck, the table at the vet's office, or just any higher surface. You don't want to hurt your back each time by trying to pick them up.

The jump command lets your dog know that you want them to get onto something, or just do a jump on the spot. While we usually teach the dog the action before adding the command word to make sure that they associate it with the right action, this is one command that we use from the get-go.

Let your dog do the *sit* cue, and hold a treat above their head just out of reach. Excitedly say "jump!", and watch what they do. Remember that your dog has no idea what you want them to do at this stage, but they will most likely try to get to the treat. If they lift their front legs off the ground, reward them.

Keep doing this at the same height a few times before increasing the height. Keep repeating the action until you can hold the treat high enough that they need to actually jump to get to it. Train them consistently so that they will start to jump on command without a treat. The next step is to lure them to the front of a platform that they can safely jump onto, and give them the command. You can hold the treat above the platform that you want them to get on to encourage them to jump onto it. This can even be your couch at home.

FETCH

A good ol' game of fetch is a great way to bond with your dog, train them, and let them get some exercise simultaneously. While some dogs don't have any problems learning to play this game, others might look at you like there's something wrong with you instead of chasing after the ball. Others will run over to the object but never bring it back. Whatever your dog is doing, you can help them learn the game with these steps.

Familiarize your dog with the ball that you want to use in your game, and let them play with it for a while. You want it to become a high-value object to them. When they've gotten to know it some, practice having them do the *drop-it* command with the toy. This may take a few tries, as your dog may become quite attached to this object.

After you've spent some time playing with the ball, you can give them the *drop-it* command, and pick it up, throwing it, but not too far. When your dog chases the ball, reward them. If they pick it up, you can also reward them. Practice the *drop-it* command after you've thrown the object a few times.

Once they trust you with the ball dropping it on command, you can throw it a bit further, and give them the *come* command when they have the ball in their mouth. You may have to do this a few times before they bring the ball with them but reward them if they do. When they bring the ball back, use the *drop-it* command to retrieve the ball. Your dog will be playing fetch with you in no time!

HOW TO PROPERLY PRAISE A DOG

As we've discussed throughout this book, praise is an integral part of positive reinforcement training. Praise is used to reinforce the behavior that you want your dog to have. We can't give our dogs a treat every time, so praise and affection will become the main ways in which we reward them for good behavior once they're well-trained.

Having a certain word like "yes" or "good" to mark when they've done something right can give you an advantage in training. When you're teaching them something that has to be taught in segments or steps, the praise word comes in handy and lets them know that they're on the right track. You can use this word as often as you like, but only when they're doing something right.

We get so caught up in life sometimes that we forget to reward our dogs for everything they do right. In order of preference, dogs like food, physical touch, and words of praise. Because physical touch is higher on the preference list than verbal praise, try to do both simultaneously when rewarding your dog.

Dogs are all unique, and some dogs might not enjoy physical touch as much due to being shy or skittish. In this case, they can be rewarded with verbal praise, and perhaps their favorite toy. You will get to know your dog and what they enjoy in due time. Remember to praise them, even when they do a command that they've been able to do for years. If the only time that they get attention is when they do something wrong, you'll be teaching them to do it more often.

Overall commands are fun to teach your dog and really come in handy in many situations. Even though it may take a lot of time, consistency, and patience, a well-trained dog is more than a joy to be around, and you won't be sorry!

CONCLUSION

> *I have found that when you are deeply troubled, there are things you get from the silent devoted companionship of a dog that you can get from no other source.*

— DORIS DAY

Raising a dog is a challenging experience. There is no doubt that you will run into some situations that will have you frustrated. However, there is no better feeling than creating a bond with your dog that will last for as long as they live.

Positive reinforcement training is the key to raising a happy, healthy, well-behaved pup. Taking a dominant stance in training your dog will do nothing but hurt your relationship. Your dog has the potential to bring you endless joy and fulfillment, and who wouldn't want that?

At the end of the day, your dog needs you just as much as you need them. Your dog needs you to step up to the plate and teach them how to fit into your home and society. They are more than willing to be loved by you, and it's all up to you to reinforce the right behavior.

Feeding your dog a healthy diet, giving them the right exercise, and potty training them are the first steps to creating a harmonious household. Your dog won't only bring joy to you but to everyone around you. Your dog depends on you to keep them safe, fed, and loved, and even if they had a choice in the matter, it wouldn't change a thing.

Dogs are pure creatures with a capacity for love and companionship that we will never quite understand to the full extent. We should never take advantage of that. Not training your dog can lead to so much frustration and problems with your relationship that some may feel that they have no choice but to give them up. In reality, all that's needed is some good positive reinforcement training and socialization.

Almost any behavioral problem that your dog may have that doesn't have clinical roots can be solved by positive reinforcement training. The day we adopt a dog, we not only take on the responsibility of feeding them and keeping them alive, but so much more than that, and we should always be ready for that commitment when we adopt.

Your dog is but a part of your life, but you *are* their entire life. They look to you for guidance, and knowing how to give them the guidance that they need is the key to a meaningful relationship.

Always remember that a healthy dog is a happy dog, and what they put into their bodies can directly affect their training and behavior. More so, each dog has a unique personality and what works for one dog won't necessarily work for another dog. We should always have the grace to understand their frustrations and emotions, just like they try to understand ours.

Positive reinforcement training is not only training for your dog but also for you. For years, the dictatorship mindset concerning pets has done so much irreparable damage to relationships and caused countless dogs to end up in the pound, abusive homes, and even worse. Once we can start thinking of them as our companions instead of something that just has to obey our will, we've unlocked the secret to happy dog ownership.

Our dogs are not our subjects, but members of the family. They are capable of feelings and emotions just like us, and they're allowed to have those feelings. Positive reinforcement training teaches us to get to know our dogs in a way that will allow us to build a strong relationship with them with love and patience.

If this book has helped you with your understanding of training and dog ownership at all, please consider leaving a review to help others just like you. The more we spread the word, the more happy pups we'll have! If you start consistently training your dog today, you will see a difference in behavior by next week. It's never too late to teach an old dog new tricks! Keep going, even when facing the challenges, and you'll reap the rewards tenfold. You have everything that you need to train your dog successfully and have a new meaningful, exciting experience each day. All that's left to do, is start!

MASTERING DOG TRAINING WITH EFFECTIVE POSITIVE REINFORCEMENT

Now that you've completed your journey through "Effective Positive Reinforcement for Dogs," you've equipped yourself with the tools to transform your dog into a well-behaved, happy companion. But why keep all this newfound wisdom to yourself?

Share the Love: Leave Your Review

Your honest opinion can guide other dog lovers to the same valuable insights you've gained. By sharing your thoughts on Amazon, you're not just reviewing a book— you're lighting the path for fellow dog enthusiasts, helping them discover the information they need to build stronger bonds with their furry friends.

Your Review Matters

Your words can make a difference in someone else's dog training journey. Imagine the impact you could have on...

- ...one more pup learning positive behaviors.
- ...one more family enjoying a harmonious relationship with their dog.
- ...one more dog owner finding effective solutions to training challenges.

How to Leave Your Review

Scan the code below to share your thoughts on Amazon:

A Heartfelt Thank You

Your support means the world to me and to dog lovers everywhere. Thank you for being a part of this community dedicated to creating happier, healthier relationships between humans and their canine companions.

Sandra FELLERS

Your Dog's Best Friend

PS - Remember, your review isn't just about the book; it's a gift to fellow dog enthusiasts seeking guidance. Let's spread the joy of effective positive reinforcement dog training together!

REFERENCES

A comprehensive guide to choosing the best dog treats. (2020, March 2). Dogsee. https://www.dogseechew.in/blog/a-comprehensive-guide-to-choosing-the-best-dog-treats

A dog's basic needs. (n.d.). Paws Chicago. https://www.pawschicago.org/news-resources/all-about-dogs/doggy-basics/a-dogs-basic-needs

Acmecanine. (2018, January 26). *5 things to use to praise with your dog.* Acme Canine. https://acmecanine.com/physical-praise/

Adams, B. W. (n.d.). *How to groom your dog at home.* The Humane Society of the United States. https://www.humanesociety.org/resources/how-groom-your-dog-home

Admin. (n.d.). *How to avoid overfeeding while training your dog.* The Good Dog Guide's Blog. https://www.thegooddogguide.com/blog/how-to-avoid-overfeeding-while-training-your-dog/

Ahern, M. (2023, July 31). *Building trust and bond: The foundation of effective dog training.* Glad Dogs Nation. https://gladdogsnation.com/blogs/blog/building-trust-and-bond-the-foundation-of-effective-dog-training

AKC Staff. (2015, August 6). *Dog training commands: Consistent dog training.* American Kennel Club. https://www.akc.org/expert-advice/training/importance-consistency-training-dog/

Andrews, P. (2022, August 31). *Make a training schedule for your dog.* The Upper Pawside. https://upperpawside.com/how-to-make-a-training-schedule-for-your-dog/

Arford, K. (2019, November 19). *Crate training benefits: Why a crate is great for you and your dog.* American Kennel Club. https://www.akc.org/expert-advice/training/why-crate-training-is-great-for-your-dog/

Argos. (2023, July 27). *Guide to dog grooming at home.* Argos Pet Insurance. https://www.argospetinsurance.co.uk/we-talk-pet/grooming-a-dog-at-home-everything-you-need-to-know/

Bauhaus, J. M. (2021a, March 12). *Choosing the right leash, collar or harness for your dog.* Hill's Pet Nutrition. https://www.hillspet.com/dog-care/routine-care/different-types-of-dog-collars-leashes-and-harnesses?lightboxfired=true#

Bauhaus, J. M. (2021b, April 23). *Medium-Sized dogs: Choosing the best breed.* Hill's Pet Nutrition. https://www.hillspet.com/dog-care/new-pet-parent/guide-to-best-medium-sized-dog-breeds?lightbox fired=true#

Becker, M. (2016, December 17). *How to teach your dog to "take it"—and why this command is so helpful.* Vetstreet. https://www.vetstreet.com/our-pet-experts/how-to-teach-your-dog-to-take-it-and-why-this-command-is-so-helpful

Bender, A. (2019, November 4). *How should you introduce a puppy to a crate?* The Spruce Pets. https://www.thesprucepets.com/get-a-puppy-used-to-a-crate-1118506

Bender, A. (2022a, April 9). *How to tell if a dog is afraid* (M. Tarantino, Ed.). The Spruce Pets. https://www.thesprucepets.com/symptoms-of-fear-in-dogs-1117890

Bender, A. (2022b, June 15). *This is how to teach your pooch how to stand on command.* The Spruce Pets. https://www.thesprucepets.com/train-your-dog-to-stand-1117299

Berger, J. (2022, December 16). *How to stop a puppy from chewing everything in sight.* Pet MD. https://www.petmd.com/dog/behavior/how-to-stop-puppy-from-chewing

Best dog food for diabetes. (n.d.). Dog Food Advisor. https://www.dogfoodadvisor.com/best-dog-foods/diabetes

Best food for dogs with arthritis. (n.d.). Dog Food Advisor. https://www.dogfoodadvisor.com/best-dog-foods/arthritis/

Bloom, I. (2023, October 17). *No more pulling! Here's how to leash train your dog.* BeChewy. https://be.chewy.com/leash-train-dog-2/

Boiko, O. (2020). *Dog begging for food: Why it happens and how to stop it.* Petfeed. https://petcube.com/blog/dog-begging-for-food/

Brain games and enrichment activities for dogs. (n.d.). Guide Dogs Site. https://www.guidedogs.org.uk/getting-support/information-and-advice/dog-care-and-welfare/dog-enrichment-ideas/

Brown, E. (2023, September 20). *Dog feeding rules by size, age, and weight.*

AZ Animals. https://a-z-animals.com/blog/dog-feeding-rules-by-size-age-and-weight/

Building a strong bond with your dog. (2023, March 2). Dogsee. https://www.dogseechew.in/blog/building-a-strong-bond-with-your-dog-importance-benefits-and-ways

Burke, A. (2023, February 3). *Understanding, preventing, and treating dog anxiety.* American Kennel Club. https://www.akc.org/expert-advice/health/treating-dog-anxiety/

Butler, S. (n.d.). *Samuel Butler quotes.* Shutterfly. https://www.shutterfly.com/ideas/dog-quotes/

Caines, K. (n.d.). *How to praise your puppy.* Dog Care - Daily Puppy. https://dogcare.dailypuppy.com/praise-puppy-2870.html

Campbell, S. (n.d.). *How to build trust with your dog.* Zoetis Petcare. https://www.zoetispetcare.com/blog/article/how-build-trust-dog

Changing habits. (n.d.). Learning Center. https://learningcenter.unc.edu/tips-and-tools/changing-habits

Chasing Tails Team. (2021, November 3). *Dog sizes: From tiny teacup to gentle giant, which should you adopt?* Chasing Tails. https://chasingtails.store/blogs/tips/dog-sizes

Checklist of dog supplies for your new fur kid. (n.d.). Nylabone. https://www.nylabone.com/dog101/checklist-of-dog-supplies-for-your-new-fur-kid

Chewing: How to stop your dog's gnawing problem. (n.d.). The Humane Society of the United States. https://www.humanesociety.org/resources/stop-your-dogs-chewing

Chewy. (2021). How to crate train a puppy [Video]. In *YouTube.* https://www.youtube.com/watch?v=Cntyy8ZImq8&t=85s&ab_channel=Chewy

Chewy Editorial. (2023a, May 9). *Potty training dogs: 9 tips for busy pet parents.* BeChewy. https://be.chewy.com/potty-training-dogs-9-tips-for-busy-pet-parents/

Chewy Editorial. (2023b, November 1). *How to teach a dog to fetch: A step-by-step guide.* BeChewy. https://be.chewy.com/how-to-teach-dog-to-fetch/

Choosing the right dog treats for your pooch. (n.d.). PupLife Dog Supplies.

https://www.puplife.com/pages/choosing-the-right-dog-treats-for-your-pooch

Conklin, M. R. (n.d.). *Dog begging for food? Here's what to do.* Zoetis Petcare. https://www.zoetispetcare.com/blog/article/dog-begging-for-food

Consistency in dog training and making the time. (2023, April 24). Pupford. https://pupford.com/consistency-dog-training/

Crate training 101. (n.d.). The Humane Society of the United States. https://www.humanesociety.org/resources/crate-training-101

Crittenden, C. (n.d.). *How to train your dog to understand "no."* Wag Walking. https://wagwalking.com/training/understand-no

Culp, C. (2014). *Top ten rules for dogs in the house.* Thriving Canine. https://www.thrivingcanine.com/blog/2014/06/25/top-ten-rules-dogs-house

Damment, E. (n.d.). *What should I feed my working dog?* Sporting Shooter. https://sporting-gun.com/article/what-should-i-feed-my-working-dog

Day, D. (n.d.). *Doris Day quotes.* Care. https://www.care.com/c/the-101-best-dog-quotes/

DeSantis, D. (2021, June 29). *How to make an outdoor dog potty area.* Puppy in Training. https://puppyintraining.com/dog-potty-area/

Destructive chewing. (n.d.). ASPCA. https://www.aspca.org/pet-care/dog-care/common-dog-behavior-issues/destructive-chewing

Dickson, P. (2023, April 27). *6 DIY indoor dog potties you can make at home (2023 update).* Hepper. https://www.hepper.com/diy-indoor-dog-potties/

Dig this: How to get your dog to stop digging. (n.d.). The Humane Society of the United States. https://www.humanesociety.org/resources/stop-dogs-digging

District Floor Depot. (2019, February 18). *Dogs and hardwood floors: How to prevent scratching.* Distrcit Floor Depot. https://www.districtfloordepot.com/blog/dogs-and-hardwood-floors-how-to-prevent-scratching/

Dog counter surfing: Prevention and deterrents. (n.d.). Best Friends Animal Society. https://resources.bestfriends.org/article/dog-counter-surfing-prevention-deterrents

Dog crates: The good, the bad, and the ugly. (n.d.). 3 Lost Dogs. https://www.3lostdogs.com/dog-crates-the-good-the-bad-and-the-ugly/

Dog training — set house rules template (download). (n.d.). Preventative Vet. https://www.preventivevet.com/dog-training-house-rules-template-download

Donovan, L. (2019, August 30). *Leash train your puppy in 5 easy steps.* American Kennel Club. https://www.akc.org/expert-advice/training/teach-puppy-walk-leash/

Dwilson, S. D. (n.d.). *How to break a dog from jumping up on the table.* Daily Puppy. https://dogcare.dailypuppy.com/break-dog-jumping-up-table-6988.html

Dylan & Rainey. (2022, April 5). *How to introduce your dog to a new home and neighborhood.* Dylan & Rainey. https://www.dylanandrainey.com/how-to-introduce-your-dog-to-a-new-home-and-neighborhood/

Eckstein, S. (2023, May 28). *Understanding why dogs bark* (A. Flowers, Ed.). WebMD. https://www.webmd.com/pets/dogs/understanding-why-dogs-bark

11 healthy, natural treats for dogs in your kitchen. (n.d.). Falls Village Vet Hospital. https://raleighncvet.com/nutrition-weight-management/11-healthy-natural-treats-for-dogs-in-your-kitchen/

Elliot, R. (2022, June 29). *Positive reinforcement training.* RSPCA Pet Insurance. https://www.rspcapetinsurance.org.au/pet-care/responsible-pet-ownership/positive-reinforcement-training

Environmental enrichment. (n.d.). Ohio State University. https://indoorpet.osu.edu/dogs/environmental_enrichment_dogs

FetchMasters. (2019, April 1). *The importance of leash training your dog.* FetchMasters. https://fetchmasters.com/importance-leash-training-dog/

5 reasons why it's important to train your dog with a dog training leash. (2022, November 8). BetterBone. https://thebetterbone.com/blogs/news/5-reasons-why-it-s-important-to-train-your-dog-with-a-dog-training-leash

5 reasons why leash training dogs is so important. (n.d.). K9 Aggression. https://k9aggression.com/5-reasons-leash-training-dogs-important/

5 reasons why pet socialization is critical. (n.d.). Longwood Veterinary Centre. https://longwoodvetcenter.com/pet-socialization-raising-a-well-adjusted-dog

Foote, S. J. (n.d.). *Dog attacks - what to do when yours is on leash and the attacker is off.* Airport Animal Hospital. https://www.aahduluth.com/index.php/seasonal-topics/34-dog-attacks-what-to-do-when-yours-is-on-leash-and-the-attacker-is-off

Friedman, K. (n.d.). *Kinky Friedman quotes.* Shutterfly. https://www.shutterfly.com/ideas/dog-quotes/

FurBabies. (2021, January 28). *Dog training - the importance of a strong bond.* Best Friends Fur Ever. https://bestfriendsfurever.com/dog-training-the-importance-of-a-strong-bond/

Garber, M. (n.d.). *Marjorie Garber quotes.* GoodReads. https://www.goodreads.com/quotes/485014-if-you-have-a-dog-you-will-most-likely-outlive

Geier, E. (n.d.). *How to introduce your rescue dog to new people.* The Dog People. https://www.rover.com/blog/introduce-rescue-dog-new-people/

Gerrity, S. (2022, August 11). *Why your dog digs—plus how to get them to stop.* Daily Paws. https://www.dailypaws.com/living-with-pets/pet-friendly-home/why-dog-digs

Gibeault, S. (2017, December 6). *Dog training for busy people: Efficient ways to train your dog.* American Kennel Club. https://www.akc.org/expert-advice/training/fit-dog-training-busy-life/

Gibeault, S. (2020a, March 17). *Grab & hold your dog's attention with the "watch me" command.* American Kennel Club. https://www.akc.org/expert-advice/training/watch-me-command-grab-dogs-attention/

Gibeault, S. (2020b, December 17). *How to teach your dog to drop it.* American Kennel Club. https://www.akc.org/expert-advice/training/teaching-your-dog-to-drop-it/

Gibeault, S. (2021a, April 20). *How to teach your dog to lie down.* American Kennel Club. https://www.akc.org/expert-advice/training/how-to-teach-your-dog-to-lie-down/

Gibeault, S. (2021b, June 16). *Positive reinforcement dog training: The science behind operant conditioning.* American Kennel Club. https://

www.akc.org/expert-advice/training/operant-conditioning-the-science-behind-positive-reinforcement-dog-training/

Gibeault, S. (2021c, August 27). *Teach your dog to stand on cue*. American Kennel Club. https://www.akc.org/expert-advice/training/teach-dog-stand-cue/

Gibeault, S. (2023, September 23). *How to teach your dog to sit*. American Kennel Club. https://www.akc.org/expert-advice/training/how-to-teach-your-dog-to-sit/

Gould, W. R. (2022, November 4). *How to teach a dog to sit: Step-by-Step*. BeChewy. https://be.chewy.com/basic-dog-training-commands-sit/

Graymore, D. (2021, August 8). *Dog training - how to make a training plan including template*. Service Dog Training School. https://www.servicedogtrainingschool.org/blog/dog-training-plan-template

Greer, M. (n.d.). *Weaning puppies off their mother - breeding tips*. Highland Pet Hospital. Retrieved October 4, 2023, from https://www.highlandpethospital.net/breeders-info/neonatal-puppy-care/weaning-and-sale

Heel - pet glossary term and definition. (n.d.). Dan's Pet Care. https://danspetcare.com/glossary/heel#:

Helping dog anxiety. (n.d.). The Humane Society of the United States. https://www.humanesociety.org/resources/separation-anxiety-dogs

Hoffmann, H. (2023, March 2). *How to potty train a puppy or adult dog* (J. Coates, Ed.). Pet MD. https://www.petmd.com/dog/general-health/how-to-potty-train-your-dog

Holgate, K. (n.d.). *Does your dog need senior dog food?* The Grey Muzzle Organization. https://www.greymuzzle.org/grey-matters/wellness/does-your-dog-need-senior-dog-food

Houellebecq, M. (n.d.). *Michel Houellebecq quotes*. BrainyQuote. https://www.brainyquote.com/quotes/michel_houellebecq_530674

House training your dog. (n.d.). Brown. https://www.brown.edu/Research/Colwill_Lab/CBP/Housetraining.htm

How much to feed your active dog. (n.d.). Eukanuba. https://www.eukanuba.com/us/articles/how-much-to-feed-your-active-dog

How to crate train your dog. (n.d.). Battersea. https://www.battersea.org. uk/pet-advice/dog-advice/how-crate-train-your-dog

How to create a feeding schedule for your dog. (2021, February 2). Wellness Pet Food. https://www.wellnesspetfood.com/blog/how-to-create-a-feeding-schedule-for-your-dog

How to get your dog to stop barking. (n.d.). The Humane Society of the United States. https://www.humanesociety.org/resources/how-get-your-dog-stop-barking

How to groom a dog: Long & short haired dogs. (n.d.). Purina. https://www. purina.co.uk/articles/dogs/health/daily-care/grooming-long-short-haired-dogs

How to introduce your pet to other people. (2018, December 14). FIGO. https://figopetinsurance.com/blog/how-introduce-your-pet-other-people

How to manage your dog's chase behaviours. (n.d.). Batter Sea. https:// www.battersea.org.uk/pet-advice/dog-advice/how-manage-your-dog%E2%80%99s-chase-behaviours

How to pick the best and safest dog toy. (n.d.). The Humane Society of the United States. https://www.humanesociety.org/resources/safe-dog-toys

How to potty train your dog or puppy. (n.d.). The Humane Society of the United States. https://www.humanesociety.org/resources/how-potty-train-your-dog-or-puppy

How to prevent dog scratches on wood floors. (n.d.). Living Spaces. https:// www.livingspaces.com/inspiration/ideas-advice/how-tos/how-to-prevent-dog-scratches-on-wood-floors

How to stop your dog barking. (n.d.). Dogs Trust. https://www.dogstrust. org.uk/dog-advice/training/unwanted-behaviours/stop-your-dog-barking

How to stop your dog from digging. (n.d.). Better Sea. https://www. battersea.org.uk/pet-advice/dog-advice/search-dog-advice/how-stop-your-dog-digging

How to successfully introduce two dogs. (n.d.). Animal Humane Society. https://www.animalhumanesociety.org/resource/how-successfully-introduce-two-dogs

How to teach your dog to walk on a lead. (n.d.). Better Sea. https://www.

battersea.org.uk/pet-advice/dog-advice/how-teach-your-dog-walk-lead

Ingraham, L. (2022, August 9). *Why socialization is so important for dogs.* Wag! https://wagwalking.com/wellness/why-socialization-is-so-important-for-dogs

Introducing your new dog to people. (2019, August). Maddie's Fund. https://www.maddiesfund.org/introducing-your-new-dog-to-people.htm

Introducing your new dog to your other dogs. (n.d.). The Humane Society of the United States. https://www.humanesociety.org/resources/introducing-new-dogs

Is your dog overheated? (n.d.). VERGI 24/7. https://www.vergi247.com/helpful-articles/is-your-dog-overheated

Joyner, L. (2022, April 26). *Here's how to teach your dog to roll over in 4 simple steps.* Country Living. https://www.countryliving.com/uk/wildlife/pets/a39796988/how-to-teach-dog-roll-over/

Kernicky, J. (n.d.). *Dog exercise needs by breed (basic guide & time chart).* Fairmount Pet Service. https://fairmountpetservice.com/Blog/pet-services-blog/dog-walking/dog-exercise-needs-breed-guide-chart/

Knapp, C. (n.d.). *Caroline Knapp quote.* A-Z Quotes. https://www.azquotes.com/quote/810048

Knapp, C. (n.d.). *Caroline Knapp quotes.* Shutterfly. https://www.shutterfly.com/ideas/dog-quotes/

Konopik, E. (n.d.). *Alternatives to choke chains, prong collars, and other aversive methods.* Animal Hospital of North Asheville. https://www.ahna.net/site/blog-asheville-vet/2020/03/30/alternatives-choke-chains-prong-collars-and-other-aversive-methods

LaFlamme, S. (2023, May 13). *Strengthening the bond of trust - the wonders of training your dog.* Linkedin. https://www.linkedin.com/pulse/strengthening-bond-trust-wonders-training-your-dog-sandra-laflamme/

Layne, M. (2023, September 13). *13 DIY indoor dog potty plans you can make today (with pictures).* Pet Keen. https://petkeen.com/diy-indoor-dog-potty-plans/

Learn how to train your dog to lie down. (n.d.). RSPCA. https://www.rspca.org.uk/adviceandwelfare/pets/dogs/training/liedown

Learn how to train your dog to sit. (n.d.). RSPCA. https://www.rspca. uk/adviceandwelfare/pets/dogs/training/sit

Leash training A puppy the right way. (2023). Rogue Pet Science. https:// roguepetscience.com/blogs/dog-training/leash-training-a-puppy

Llera, R., & Yuill, C. (n.d.). *Nutrition - general feeding guidelines for dogs.* VCA Animal Hospitals. https://vcahospitals.com/know-your-pet/ nutrition-general-feeding-guidelines-for-dogs

London, K. B. (2014, January 4). *Teach your dog to "back up."* The Wildest. https://www.thewildest.com/dog-behavior/teaching-dogs-back

Lotz, K. (2023, February 23). *How often should you wash your dog?* American Kennel Club. https://www.akc.org/expert-advice/health/ how-often-should-you-wash-your-dog/

Lowrey, S. (2020, August 11). *How to teach your dog to fetch.* American Kennel Club. https://www.akc.org/expert-advice/training/teach-your-dog-to-fetch/

Lowrey, S. (2021, November 8). *Small training sessions make a big impact: Dog training ideas for busy people.* American Kennel Club. https:// www.akc.org/expert-advice/training/small-training-sessions-train ing-ideas-for-busy-people/

Lowrey, S. (2022, August 26). *How to stop leash tugging and biting when walking.* American Kennel Club. https://www.akc.org/expert-advice/training/solutions-for-dogs-that-tug-on-leashes

LTHQ. (2020, January 9). *Set house rules for your dog or puppy before getting them home.* Labrador Training HQ. https://www.labrador traininghq.com/labrador-puppies/set-some-house-rules-before-you-get-your-puppy-home/

Maciejewski, K. (2018, January 19). *How to train your dog to not jump on the table.* Wag! https://wagwalking.com/training/not-jump-on-the-table

Madson, C. (2019, March 9). *Choosing the best dog crate for your dog and your life.* Preventive Vet. https://www.preventivevet.com/dogs/ how-to-measure-and-choose-a-dog-crate

Mansourian, E. (2021, August 15). *Puppy feeding fundamentals.* American Kennel Club. https://www.akc.org/expert-advice/health/ puppy-feeding-fundamentals/

March, P. (2015, December 4). *Top 5 tips for teething puppies.* DVM 360.

https://www.dvm360.com/view/top-5-tips-teething-puppies

MasterClass. (2022a, May). *How much water should a dog drink?* MasterClass. https://www.masterclass.com/articles/how-much-water-should-a-dog-drink

MasterClass. (2022b, June 8). *Why do dogs scratch the floor? 4 tips to stop dog scratching.* MasterClass. https://www.masterclass.com/articles/why-do-dogs-scratch-the-floor

MasterClass. (2022c, June 16). *How often should I take my dog out? 3 factors to consider.* MasterClass. https://www.masterclass.com/articles/how-often-should-i-take-my-dog-out

McClure, E., & Ulbrich, B. (2022, September 5). *How to build an outdoor dog potty area on concrete.* WikiHow. https://www.wikihow.com/Build-an-Outdoor-Dog-Potty-Area-on-Concrete

Meyers, H. (2019, September 30). *Puppy potty training schedule: A timeline for housebreaking your puppy.* American Kennel Club. https://www.akc.org/expert-advice/training/potty-training-your-puppy-timeline-and-tips/

Meyers, H. (2022, September 29). *Trim your dog's nails safely: Tips, tricks, and grooming techniques.* American Kennel Club. https://www.akc.org/expert-advice/health/how-to-trim-dogs-nails-safely/

Miller, D. B. (2019, September 22). *Dog feeding schedule: Why it's important and how to do it.* Top Dog Tips. https://topdogtips.com/dog-feeding-schedule/

Miller, P. (2017, September 19). *Great solutions for dog crate problems.* Whole Dog Journal. https://www.whole-dog-journal.com/training/crates/great-solutions-for-dog-crate-problems/

Miller, P. (2020, December 21). *Dog house rules.* Whole Dog Journal. https://www.whole-dog-journal.com/behavior/dog-house-rules/

Nelson, M. (2021, May 26). *How to introduce your dog to its new home: 8 steps (with pictures).* WikiHow. https://www.wikihow.com/Introduce-Your-Dog-to-Its-New-Home

Niscole. (2021, March 6). *6 tips to stop your dog from overeating.* Fitbark. https://www.fitbark.com/blog/6-tips-to-stop-your-dog-from-overeating

Nubialopezroman. (n.d.). *Homemade doggy potty.* Instructables. https://www.instructables.com/homemade-doggy-potty/

Nutrition & feeding: Dogs. (n.d.). Hill's Pet Nutrition. https://www.hill spet.co.za/dog-care/nutrition-feeding

Outdoor dog potty area: How to build one in 2023. (2023, April 8). Happy Oodles. https://happyoodles.com/2020/07/dog-potty-area-ideas-and-tips/

Paretts, S. P. (2022, March 6). *Crates for dogs: How to choose the best dog crate.* American Kennel Club. https://www.akc.org/expert-advice/lifestyle/choose-best-crate-dog/

Parlin, K. (2023, June 12). *11 tips for how to introduce dogs to new people and other dogs.* Care. https://www.care.com/c/11-tips-on-how-to-introduce-dogs-to-new-peopl/

Parrish, C. (2023, October 13). *Buying guide: How to choose the best dog crate for your pet.* BeChewy. https://be.chewy.com/dog-crate-buying-guide/

PAWS. (n.d.). *How to crate train your dog.* PAWS. https://www.paws.org/resources/how-to-crate-train-your-dog/

Pet Pro Supply Co. (2019, December 19). *How long is too long to crate your dog?* Pet pro Supply Co. https://petprosupplyco.com/blogs/blog/how-long-is-too-long-to-crate-your-dog

PetMD Editorial. (2020, March 18). *How to introduce dogs the right way* (A. Gerken & V. Schade, Eds.). PetMD. https://www.petmd.com/dog/training/evr_introducing_a_new_dog_to_a_resident_dog

Positive reinforcement—training with rewards. (n.d.). Dogs Trust. https://www.dogstrust.org.uk/dog-advice/training/techniques/positive-reinforcement-training-with-rewards

Potts, K. (2014, September 5). *New study reveals the best way to praise a dog.* Woman's Day. https://www.womansday.com/life/pet-care/news/a48993/new-study-reveals-the-best-way-to-praise-a-dog/

Potty training for pooches: How to create a comfortable and effective. (n.d.). Porch Potty USA. https://porchpotty.com/blogs/news/potty-training-for-pooches-how-to-create-a-comfortable-and-effective-potty-spot-for-your-dog

Primal Pet Foods. (2017, December 22). *Why it is important to feed your pet on a schedule.* Primal Pet Foods. https://primalpetfoods.com/blogs/news/why-it-is-important-to-feed-your-pet-on-a-schedule

Puppy Leaks. (2019, March 27). *3 easy ways to stop your dog from begging.* Puppy Leaks. https://www.puppyleaks.com/dog-from-begging/

Rabideau, C. (2020, May 28). *20 must-have products for new dog owners.* USA Today. https://www.usatoday.com/story/tech/reviewedcom/2020/05/28/20-must-have-products-new-dog-owners/111876242/

Radner, G. (n.d.). *Gilda Radner quotes.* BrainyQuote. https://www.brainyquote.com/quotes/gilda_radner_843224

Rain, K. (2022, January 22). *Is it better to walk your dog on a collar or a harness?* The Daily Wag. https://wagwalking.com/daily/is-it-better-to-walk-your-dog-on-a-collar-or-a-harness

Reisen, J. (2021, March 1). *How to create house rules for your new puppy.* American Kennel Club. https://www.akc.org/expert-advice/training/how-to-create-house-rules-for-your-new-puppy/#:

Remp, E. (2023, May 1). *Which type of dog food bowl is best for your dog?* BARK Post. https://post.bark.co/products/dog-food-bowl-guide

Roth, C. (2020, July 24). *Choosing the correct collar and leash for your pet.* Pets Best. https://www.petsbest.com/blog/choosing-correct-collar-leash-for-pet

S, P. (n.d.). *What can I freeze for my teething puppy?* Dog Temperament. https://dogtemperament.com/what-to-freeze-for-teething-puppy/

Schade, V. (2018, January 22). *The power of praise: Encouraging good behavior in dogs.* Pet MD. https://www.petmd.com/dog/behavior/power-praise-encouraging-good-behavior-dogs

Schade, V. (2023, October 10). *How to crate train a dog: Step-by-Step instructions.* BeChewy. https://be.chewy.com/how-to-crate-train-a-puppy-a-step-by-step-guide-from-an-expert/

Senic, B. (2020, September 8). *Feeding Pets with Pancreatitis.* Hill's Veterinary Nutrition Blog. https://www.myhillsvet.com.au/blog/feeding-pets-with-pancreatitis/

Sharpe, S. (2021, November 5). *How to crate train your dog in 9 easy steps.* American Kennel Club. https://www.akc.org/expert-advice/training/how-to-crate-train-your-dog-in-9-easy-steps/

Shutterfly Community. (2023, February 15). *80+ dog quotes and captions.* Shutterfly. https://www.shutterfly.com/ideas/dog-quotes/

6 steps to teaching your dog to fetch. (2020, September 14). Cesar's Way.

https://www.cesarsway.com/6-steps-to-teaching-your-dog-to-fetch/

Skaya Siberian. (2021). The EASIEST way to teach your dog to ROLL OVER! | how to teach your dog to roll over [Video]. In *YouTube*. https://www.youtube.com/watch?v=IsJ0VdeOJcg

Small Door's Medical Experts. (n.d.). *Puppy 101: Positive reinforcement training*. Small Door Veterinary. https://www.smalldoorvet.com/learning-center/puppies-kittens/positive-reinforcement-training

Small Door's medical experts. (n.d.). *Exercise needs for puppies, adults and senior dogs*. Small Door Veterinary. https://www.smalldoorvet.com/learning-center/wellness/exercise-needs-dog-lifestages

Smith, A. (2021). *Dogs counter surfing: Causes and solutions on how to stop*. Petfeed. https://petcube.com/blog/dog-stealing-food/

Smith, C.-L. (2021, January 8). *How to train your dog to jump on command*. Wag Walking. https://wagwalking.com/training/jump-on-command

Smith, T. (n.d.). *The importance of potty training a puppy*. Luv My Sitter. https://luvmysitter.com/the-importance-of-potty-training-a-puppy/

Socializing your dog. (n.d.). Animal Humane Society. https://www.animalhumanesociety.org/resource/socializing-your-dog

Stregowski, J. (2020, January 20). *How to care for your dog's basic needs*. The Spruce Pets. https://www.thesprucepets.com/your-dogs-basic-needs-1117433

Sung, W. (2019, August 6). *Dog fear and anxiety - how to calm an anxious dog*. PetMD. https://www.petmd.com/dog/conditions/behavioral/c_dg_fears_phobia_anxiety

Svoboda, M. (2021, June 3). *Quotes of famous people*. Quote Park. https://quotepark.com/quotes/1028942-marjorie-garber-if-you-have-a-dog-you-will-most-likely-outlive-it/

Teach your dog to walk on a loose leash. (n.d.). Animal Humane Society. https://www.animalhumanesociety.org/resource/teach-your-dog-walk-loose-leash

Teaching a dog to look at you. (2019, July 6). Cesar's Way. https://www.cesarsway.com/train-your-dog-to-look-at-you/

Teaching your dog to "speak" on command. (2023, June 27). BatterSea.

https://www.battersea.org.uk/pet-advice/dog-advice/teaching-your-dog-speak-command

10 commands to teach your dog. (2019, June 18). DOGUE. https://www.dogue.com.au/blogs/posts/10-commands-to-teach-your-dog

10 dog breeds prone to anxiety and how to help them. (2022, February 7). Rufus & Coco Australia. https://rufusandcoco.com.au/blogs/blog/10-dog-breeds-prone-to-anxiety-and-how-to-help-them

The basic needs of your dog. (n.d.). Authentica Petfoods. https://www.authenticapets.com/en/blog/the-basic-needs-of-your-dog

The benefits of crate training. (n.d.). PAWS. https://www.paws.org/resources/the-benefits-of-crate-training/

The benefits of omega-3 and omega-6 for dogs. (n.d.). Purina. https://www.purina.ca/articles/dog/nutrition/benefits-omega-3-and-omega-6-dogs

The benefits of socializing your dog. (n.d.). Reed Animal Hospital. https://www.reedanimalhospital.com/blog/the-benefits-of-socializing-your-dog/

The Farmer's Dog. (2021, March 13). *How much exercise do dogs need?* The Farmer's Dog. https://www.thefarmersdog.com/digest/how-much-exercise-do-dogs-need/

The importance of protein in dog food - Iams. (n.d.). Iams US. https://www.iams.com/dog/dog-articles/why-your-dog-needs-protein

The role of fat in canine nutrition. (n.d.). Purina pro Club. https://www.purinaproclub.com/resources/dog-articles/nutrition/bettering-the-breed/the-role-of-fat-in-canine-nutrition

3 ways to effectively potty train your puppy. (n.d.). Dogtopia. https://www.dogtopia.com/blog/3-ways-effectively-potty-train-puppy/

Tips on how to potty train your dog or puppy. (n.d.). The Humane Society of the United States. https://www.humanesociety.org/resources/how-potty-train-your-dog-or-puppy#:

Todd, Z. (2013, July 31). The importance of food in dog training. *Companion Animal Psychology.* https://www.companionanimalpsychology.com/2013/07/the-importance-of-food-in-dog-training.html

Tolle, E. (2018, October 9). *Eckhart Tolle quotes.* Shutterfly. https://www.shutterfly.com/ideas/dog-quotes/

Train your dog: The relevance of consistency! (2018, January 8). Tractive. https://tractive.com/blog/en/training-en/consistency-and-rituals-in-dog-training

Training "stay" vs. "wait." (n.d.). Cornell University College of Veterinary Medicine. https://www.vet.cornell.edu/departments-centers-and-institutes/riney-canine-health-center/canine-health-information/training-stay-vs-wait

Trott, S. (2021, September 9). *How to help your dog adjust to a new environment.* Now Fresh. https://nowfresh.com/en/help-your-dog-adjust-to-a-new-environment

Tupler, T. (2021, February 1). *What's in a balanced dog food?* PetMD. https://www.petmd.com/dog/nutrition/evr_dg_whats_in_a_balanced_dog_food

Use 7 simple dog training tips to teach a dog no. (2023, July 3). Dog's Best Life. https://dogsbestlife.com/dog-training/teach-a-dog-no/?cn-reloaded=1

Using food to train your dog. (n.d.). Canine Engineering. https://canineengineering.com/using-food-to-train-your-dog/

Vanbeselaere, B. (2020, January 27). *A dog's feeding schedule: When and how often to feed your dog.* Edgard & Cooper. https://www.edgardcooper.com/en/blog/a-dogs-feeding-schedule-how-often-should-i-feed-my-dog-in-a-day/

Vuckovic, A., & Popyk, Y. (2021). *Dog chewing everything? Here is how to stop them!* Petfeed. https://petcube.com/blog/stop-dog-chewing/

Wagner, R. (n.d.). *Robert Wagner quotes.* Shutterfly. https://www.shutterfly.com/ideas/dog-quotes/

Ware, E. (n.d.). *12 things you can do to quiet a barking dog.* Wedgewood Pharmacy. https://www.wedgewoodpharmacy.com/blog/posts/12-things-you-can-do-to-quiet-a-barking-dog.html

WebMD Editorial Contributors. (2021, July 7). *How to choose a dog collar* (V. Farmer, Ed.). WebMD. https://www.webmd.com/pets/dogs/how-to-choose-a-dog-collar

WebMD Editorial Contributors. (2023, July 17). *How to prevent a dog from digging* (K. Claussen, Ed.). WebMD. https://www.webmd.com/pets/dogs/how-to-prevent-a-dog-from-digging

Wells, B. (2016). *Dog separation anxiety: Definition, symptoms, causes, treatment.* Petfeed. https://petcube.com/blog/dog-separation-anxiety/

What happens if you don't groom your dog: An interview with Quinci Cole. (2023, June 2). Pupford. https://pupford.com/what-happens-if-dont-groom-dog/

What is positive reinforcement? (n.d.). Victoria Stilwell Positively. https://positively.com/dog-training/positive-training/positive-reinforcement/

What is small breed dog food? (n.d.). Dragonfly Products. https://dragonflyproducts.co.uk/blogs/help-advice/what-is-the-difference-between-small-breed-dog-food-and-standard-dog-food

When can puppies eat dry food? – beco. (n.d.). Beco Pets. https://www.becopets.com/blogs/news/when-can-puppies-eat-dry-food

When to switch puppy to dog food. (n.d.). Purina. https://www.purina.ca/articles/puppy/feeding/when-to-switch-to-adult-dog-food

Where should my dog sleep at night time? (2023, April 19). Tractive. https://tractive.com/blog/en/good-to-know/where-should-your-dog-sleep

Whether you're training a puppy or teaching your older dog new tricks, find out how a schedule can help build their skills faster. (n.d.). Thrive Pet Healthcare. https://www.thrivepetcare.com/thrive-guide/how-to-implement-a-dog-training-schedule

Which vitamins and minerals do dogs need? (2022, March 22). Care First Animal Hospital. https://www.carefirstanimalhospital.com/news-events/which-vitamins-and-minerals-do-dogs-need

Why does my dog pull on the leash? (2022, July 17). The Dog Wizard. https://thedogwizard.com/blog/why-does-my-dog-pull-on-the-leash/

Williams, K., & Downing, R. (n.d.). *Feeding the pregnant dog.* VCA Animal Hospitals. https://vcahospitals.com/know-your-pet/feeding-the-pregnant-dog

Yong, E. (2016, June 2). *The origin of dogs: When, where, and how many times were they domesticated?* The Atlantic. https://www.theatlantic.com/science/archive/2016/06/the-origin-of-dogs/484976/